open

W0082615

open

open

editorial

JORINDE SEIJDEL

BEYOND PRIVACY
NEW PERSPECTIVES ON THE PUBLIC
AND PRIVATE DOMAINS

Privacy is a defensive right that
protects a person's private life.
However, the 'right to be left
alone' is not just a legal but also
a political and social construction.
Therefore, this is a concept that,
although established by law, can be
experienced and observed differently
by individuals and groups, depending
upon their position in society and
the desires and interests attend-
ant upon that. For instance, privacy
can be an urgent topic for civil
rights movements, whereas citizens
apparently are less bothered about
it. And so more and more government
measures can be taken and new technologies applied that conflict with
the right of privacy but which are
used in a relatively unconcerned way
or submitted to with hardly a whis-
per of protest.

Whether this be an endangered
basic right, an obsolete concept of
the enlightenment, a lost cause or an
activists' obsession, the traditional
notion of privacy has largely been
undermined in today's security and
information society. This certainly
is the result of a preventive government policy that is out to control the
comings and goings of citizens, and a
commercial sector that, off-line and
online, tries to get more and more of
a handle on the individual desires
and consumption patterns of customers through its clever registration
devices. But there is more going on:
people are having less and less qualms
about voluntarily revealing personal
information in the media and on the
Internet. The protection of privacy
seems to be subordinate to people's
desire to manifest themselves publically in society. In the globalized
network cultures, visibility, transparency, accessibility and connectivity are what count. These values are
at odds with the idea of privacy as
'secluded from the rest'. Does this
imply that 'everyone belongs to everyone else' to an increasing extent, as
in Huxley's dystopic *Brave New World*
(1932)? Or, these many years after *The
Fall of Public Man* (Richard Sennett,
1974) are we experiencing 'the fall
of private man' – from which we could
then conclude that the public-private
antithesis has lost its force as a
signifier of meaning? Are alternative
subjectivities and rights emerging
that are considered more important
in the twenty-first century? Are new
strategies and tactics being mobilized to safeguard personal autonomy
and to escape forms of institutional
biopower?

In *Open* 19, the concept of privacy is examined and reconsidered
from different perspectives: legal,

sociological, media theoretical and activist. Rather than deploring the loss of privacy, the main focus is on the attempt, starting from our present position of 'post-privacy', to gain an idea of what is on the horizon in terms of new subjectivities and power constructions. Naturally, this cannot be investigated without paying attention to the sociopolitical and technological violations of privacy that are going on at present.

Daniel Solove, law professor, proposes that privacy be considered as a pluralistic concept with a social significance. A theory on privacy should be directed at the very problems that create a need for privacy, according to Solove. Maurizio Lazzarato, taking Foucault's concept of 'pastoral power' as an example, analyses how the state wields power techniques to control the users of social services, and how it intervenes in the lives of individuals in doing so. Sociologist Rudi Laermans goes into the implications of the ideal of transparent communication for secrecy and personal privacy.

In search of effective strategies against the surveillance regime, Armin Medosch, media artist and researcher, has developed a model in which he couples the historical function of privacy in a free democracy with the overall technopolitical dynamics. Felix Stalder examines today's 'post-privacy' situation, in which a change is taking place in how people achieve autonomy, and how institutions and corporations exercise control over them.

In the column, Joris van Hoboken, member of the board at Bits of Freedom, challengingly states: 'Privacy is dead. Get over it.' Oliver Leistert uses a post-Fordian framework in criticizing the German protest movement AK-Vorrat, which focuses on issues concerning data retention and privacy from a liberal democratic standpoint. Martijn de Waal considers the concrete possibilities of using locational data from cellular networks for civil society projects and the questions on privacy that this raises. In the light of contemporary computer paradigms like the Internet of Things, Rob van Kranenburg argues in favour of making concepts of privacy operational from the bottom up in the infrastructure of technologies and networks that connect us with one another in our environment.

Mark Shepard has made a contribution on 'The Sentient City Survival Kit', his research project in the area of design, which proposes playful and ironic technosocial artefacts that investigate the consequences that the observing, evermore efficiently and excessively coded city has for privacy and autonomy. Matthijs Bouw, architect and director of One Architecture, investigates privatization and privacy in the context of the Internet platform 'New Map of Tbilisi'. With photos by Gio Sumbadze and Lucas Zoutendijk, he shows how the 'wild capitalism' of the new Georgia has led to a reduction of privacy in Tbilisi.

Editorial

Rudi Laermans

Communicative

Sovereignty

The import of the pair of concepts 'public and private', long considered the expression of an architectural fundamental truth, has expanded, even become existential, with the rise of modern methods of communication. Owing to the fact that private life has become completely interwoven with the (digital) outside world, the concept of privacy in this day and age holds many paradoxes. According to Belgian sociologist Rudi Laermans, the need for a 'no man's land', free of all interchange, beyond or beside the law, is only the greater for this.

'Whereof one cannot speak, thereof one must be silent.'
(Wittgenstein, once again)

Inside/Outside

'An indoor business, a matter of events that take place behind closed doors and under lock and key, private life might seem to be walled off from prying eyes,' writes the French historian Georges Duby in his foreword to *A History of Private Life*, a five-volume series spanning a period of over two millennia.[1] Duby alludes to the etymology of the Latin word *privatus*, which among other things means 'secluded' and 'free of', and simultaneously affirms the accepted view of the distinction between private and public life: the first takes place indoors, the second outdoors. Between the indoor and outdoor space are walls, partitions that shelter and protect but never only take the form of closures. Windows provide visual contact with the surroundings outside the space, doors open and shut: they enable interchanges between inside and outside. Precisely because it can be opened, a closed door gives a stronger feeling of seclusion than an undifferentiated wall. At the same time, it symbolizes the possibility of breaking through the boundary of the private sphere at any moment and 'socializing', as the expression goes. We are boundary-goers who separate in order to connect: we erect a material boundary

1. Georges Duby, 'Foreword to A History of Private Life', in: Paul Veyne (ed.), *A History of Private Life 1: From Pagan Rome to Byzantium* (Boston: Harvard University Press, 1987), viii.

in stone or concrete between indoors and outdoors, but do not live in a prison. In recognition of that fact, the German philosopher and sociologist Georg Simmel gives a semi-metaphysical interpretation of the phenomenon of the door at the end of his essay 'Bridge and Door': 'Just as the formless limitation takes on a shape, its limitedness finds its significance and dignity only in that which the mobility of the door illustrates: in the possibility at any moment of stepping out of the limitation into freedom.'[2]

The topological view of the difference between private and public is essentially architectural. Architecture, both as a design practice and theoretical construct, never works exclusively with a neutral, purely mathematically defined space, but always presupposes the possibility of a qualitative dichotomy between inside and outside. 'Doing architecture' means differentiating between an inside and outside; therefore, the basic medium of architecture is the screen, which assumes the form of a closure (the wall), an opening (the window) or both (the door). Inside/outside is the fundamental differential for all architecture, its universal basic model to which it gives form, and which design practice continually repeats and shifts, quotes and varies. Architecture can be designed and presented in countless ways, but 'you know it is architecture only when you can go inside and come back out again, and when the relations change with this going-inside-and-coming-

2. Georg Simmel, 'Bridge and Door', *Theory, Culture & Society*, vol. 11 (1994) no. 1, 10.

back-out; in other words, something different happens and can be expected inside than outside'.[3] However, the combination of the difference between inside and outside with the private/public distinction no longer expresses an architectural

3. Dirk Baecker, 'Die Dekonstruktion der Schachtel: Innen und Aussen in der Architektur', in: Niklas Luhmann, Frederick D. Bunsen and Dirk Baecker, *Unbeoabachtbare Welt: Über Kunst und Architektur* (Bielefeld: Haux, 1990), 83.

but an existential basic truth: man is an animal that makes a home for himself by giving his body an imaginary extension, projecting it in a space that s/he can call 'my own'. A home presupposes architecture, but is essentially a form of body culture and, all things considered, a curious mixture of naked biological life and civilization.

The Postmodern Living Capsule

The twentieth century thoroughly overturned man's being-in-the-world by making residence explicit. The modernist movement redefined the home as an abstract function with basic variables and thus took it out of the domain of the self-evident, and also out of the domain of social standing and representation. The most important design outcome was the generic apartment block, which undoubtedly will also remain the dominant type of housing in the future. It is the breeding ground of the present-day 'apartment individualism' as well. In the last part of his trilogy *Spheres*, Peter Sloterdijk uses this neologism to crystallize one of the basic intuitions in his diagnosis of the present era. According to him,

today's individualism combines a psychological-mental attitude with an entirety of place-specific self-practices aimed at self-stimulation and self-indulgence. The private spatial sphere therefore has transformed into a comfortable 'egosphere' or 'self container', the individual home into 'a spatial immune system', 'a defensive measure by which an area of well-being is closed to intruders and other bringers of nausea'.[4] There is a word for this hypertrophying of the private sphere: cocooning. The

4. Peter Sloterdijk, *Sphären III: Schäume* (Frankfurt am Main: Suhrkamp, 2004), 535.

expression sounds dated now, but in the rich West or the 'internal space of world capital' (Sloterdijk) cocooning remains a dominant trend. The fact that we are hearing less talk of this only proves that by now the trend has morphed into a generalized condition of life. Cocooning is the expression at the social micro level of the more general process of 'foaming' (Sloterdijk) or 'capsularizing' (De Cauter). Indeed, the longer the more, we live in a society that resembles a gigantic chain of mutually isolated bubbles or capsules piled atop one another. As Lieven de Cauter notes in 'The Capsule and the Network': 'We could come up with a whole range of new spaces that are capsular. We could call the capsular house a *cocoon*, and self-contained complexes (airports, shopping malls, all-in hotels) could be designated *envelopes*, leaving the term *enclave* for theme parks, shopping streets and ghettos.'[5]

5. Lieven De Cauter, 'The Capsule and the Network: Notes for a General Theory', in: Lieven De Cauter, *The Capsular Civilization: On the City in the Age of Fear* (Rotterdam: NAi Publishers, 2005).

From the German philosopher Leibniz comes the idea that we live in the best of all possible worlds: 'Tout est pour le mieux dans le meilleur des mondes possibles.' From the cosmological point of view the expression seems implausible, but it is made to measure for the way in which the standard living capsule is experienced by its occupant(s). This is indeed a special type of *machine à habiter*. The domestic cocoon is simultaneously a conservatory with a relatively constant climate, a high-tech wellness centre and a junction of virtual lines of communication that can be actualized at any moment. Previously, the home was a social isolation cell for the nuclear family, which generally maintained a highly selective entrance policy at the front door; now, it is no longer a social ignorance machine but a communicative cockpit, an 'inside' in which one withdraws from direct, physically-based contact with others with an eye to more indirect communication through various forms of media. The ego oriented to self-stimulation wants to control communication with others as much as possible and therefore prefers to look at the messages of others on a television or computer screen than to confront the direct gaze of a stranger in physical public space. The imaginary 'Other' is no longer an unfathomable being but the virtual world of information possibilities that one can log into from the living capsule (there also is a new 'Real Other': the enigmatic operating program, the underlying code and algorithms with which one navigates in the digital world).

The paradoxical enclosure of the barred social outside in the private inside has two preconditions. The first concerns the outdoor space or environment: it is reduced to a collection of contactable addresses and a multiple information provider. The information that is brought inside often is about 'the outside', even the most immediate surroundings. For example, someone wanting to know exactly what the weather is like does not look out the window or step outside the door but consults the much more exact information provided by the local meteorological institute on the Internet. The second precondition concerns the indoor space: it is used as a communications control room. The dwelling capsule is a multiple receptor, a terminal of words, images and sounds that can be called up and removed, cherished and forgotten (and then eventually reactivated) by the resident(s) at will. When the available information channels also offer possibilities to answer or interact, they are likewise highly selectively utilized in accordance with the wishes of one's own self. The spatial isolation of the home is especially prized because it offers rest, permits an often absent-minded submergence of the self in the stream of information under consideration. The couch potato and the nerd are the new psychophysical ideal types that everybody laughs at because they represent the extreme poles of a scale on which they themselves also hold a position.

Communicative Sovereignty

The contemporary subject is a multiple sovereign. The traditional spatial privacy within the home generates a modest – and both legally and biopolitically constricted, although not less real – form of territorial sovereignty. It is also the habitat of actions that to a certain extent imitate the public life of the state: individually or together with a life companion making (house) rules, setting up design budgets, formulating priorities for the midterm . . . Nowadays, territorial sovereignty in the dwelling-place is especially valued for its symbiosis with the communicative sovereignty offered by various forms of telecommunications. One can sovereignly connect to the mass media and zap away like the King of the Kingdom, in the full awareness that individual choices are indirectly steered by social determinants. Those who log into the offerings of the mass media voluntarily become members of a primarily passive audience, regardless of the fact that it regularly sends its more active representatives to various sorts of reality television. This audience has no physical contours but only exists as a temporary attention community that is spread over countless points in space and continuously in *statu nascendi*. Here you have the postmodern social order in a nutshell: no question of a substantial integration on the basis of collectively shared norms or values, but a floating, incessantly remade instant integration within networks of mass communication, thanks to the short-lived collective attention for sensational themes. Its herald is not Guy Debord, who in *La Société du Spectacle* still thinks too much in terms of false 'appearance' and authentic 'being', but rather the German sociologist Niklas Luhmann. As early as 1975, Luhmann observed that the 'primary social function' of the mass media 'lies in the participation of all in a common reality, or more precisely, in the creation of such an impression, which then imposes itself as operative fiction and becomes reality'.[6]

In the private sphere, one can also turn against the receptive passivity of the mass media and opt for the interactivity of the Internet and other digital information possibilities. Whatever the motive for this – intellectual snobbery or, on the contrary, the simple need as an intellectual flex worker to stay informed (what exactly is the difference?) – people want to have communicative autonomy. Both modes – passivity (the mass media) and interactivity (telephony, the Internet) – are governed by the sovereign ability to refuse, receive and send information. The hyper-individualized subject cherishes this communicative sovereignty and values territorial sovereignty within the home largely as a precondition to that. Traditionally, thanks to screening off, spatial privacy was synonymous with refusing possibilities for communication, with saying 'no' to the self's inescapable

6. Niklas Luhmann, 'Veränderungen im System gesellschaftlicher Kommunikation und die Massenmedien', in: Niklas Luhmann, *Soziologische Aufklärung 3: Soziales System, Gesellschaft, Organisation* (Opladen: Westdeutscher Verlag, 1981), 320.

transformation into a source of visual information or potential verbal communication when in physical public space. The 'no' to public life generally went together with a greatly reduced social 'yes': inside the home, communication remained limited to eventual housemates and invited friends or acquaintances who dropped by. Conversely, the structural coupling of the home with network space has created a virtual social world of optional telecommunications that positively redefines the earlier refusal to communicate. The digital revolution is the temporary endpoint of this transformation. We 'postmoderns' can lead a sovereign social life within doors that does not shut out but includes a broad range of contacts out of doors. Private life no longer means only minimal or zero sociability, but is becoming completely interwoven with an often complex network sociality. 'Sociability' is nonverbal and verbal communication in a situation of physical co-presence, or the interaction between people who are physically present; 'sociality' is telecommunications, or the passive or interactive connection with people who are not physically present. In the postmodern age, sociality dominates sociability, while communicative sovereignty dominates territorial sovereignty. The postmodern subject remains physically interactive, naturally, but is above all 'connective'; he or she indeed still maintains direct relationships, but primarily has network contacts. Descartes gave to modernity the adage 'Cogito ergo sum', which is fitting for a highly introverted, inward-directed private existence; postmodernism recognizes itself in the as-yet-unclaimed motto, 'I exist because I am connected'.

Secret

The Modern Movement in architecture made residence reflexive; the digital revolution, which has pressed ahead without a self-appointed avant-garde, exposes the hard core of both individual privacy and private life: keeping information about oneself secret when communicating with others. The French historian Gérard Vincent is right when he calls the secret the 'red thread' in the history of private life – not the total secret, which by definition leaves no traces, but the shifting boundary between what is said and what is not, according to time and place.[7] The etymology of the French and English word 'secret', like that of the word 'privacy', brings us to the idea of seclusion. 'Secret' refers to the Latin 'secretus', the past participle of the verb 'secerno', which means to separate or seclude. The personal secret does not entirely seclude an individual from the public sphere, but introduces a separation within the whole of possible communications about oneself. Certain information about the self is structurally isolated as incommunicable from all other, communicable information. The separation procedure in principle takes little effort, for simply not communi-

7. Gérard Vincent, 'Een geschiedenis van het geheim?', in: Antoine Prost and Gérard Vincent (eds.), *Geschiedenis van het persoonlijk leven 5: Van de Eerste Wereldoorlog tot onze tijd* (Amsterdam: Agon, 1990), 147.

cating is sufficient: withholding information is a form of remaining silent. The unspoken information remains 'inside', with the individual whose personal life is also the subject matter of the information. This is why Georg Simmel calls secrets 'inner private property' in the detailed chapter that he devotes to 'the secret and the secret society' in his *Soziologie* (1907).[8]

The personal secret is private in a double sense: it is about someone's private life, and it is secluded and guarded within it. Partly for this reason, personal secrets form the essence of a person's private life. They can refer to actions that a person only carries out in a situation of social isolation, but also include thoughts, desires, emotions . . . (which by definition are a private matter: every human consciousness is an impenetrable black box for others). The information about one's own self that is not shared or shared only with one or two others, is in the final instance a possible truth about that self. A personal secret is an intimate truth that must remain concealed because it can embarrass, socially discredit or disgrace an individual. By no means is it always about forbidden desires, taboo ideas or deviant behaviour. The mass media employ this limited definition of the personal secret. They have latched onto and spread the idea that secret information is always sen-

8. Georg Simmel, 'Das Geheimnis und die geheime Gesellschaft', in: Georg Simmel, *Soziologie: Untersuchungen über die Formen der Vergesellschaftung* (Frankfurt am Main: Suhrkamp, 1992), 383-455. Partial English translation: Georg Simmel, 'Secrecy', in: Kurt H. Wolff (ed.), *The Sociology of Georg Simmel* (New York: The Free Press, 1950), 330-376.

sational, whereas personal secrets are often of a more prosaic nature. The outwardly decisive manager who frequently hesitates in making necessary decisions and sometimes simply does not know what to do, also has a personal secret. The informational value of the personal secret does not lie in the contents of the information itself but in the social effect that its eventual exposure would produce.

Speaking/Remaining Silent

'If human sociation is conditioned by the capacity to speak, it is shaped by the capacity to be silent,' commented Simmel in one of the rare footnotes in his *Soziologie*.[9] It is an apt observation, shattering with one well-aimed blow the present-day fixation on communication, transparency and *une parole vraie*. To be sure, man is a talking animal that, *pace* Heidegger, prefers the oblivion within the babble of the 'one' to an authentic existence. But a being that speaks can also consciously choose mutism. According to the Canadian sociologist Erving Goffman, who in *The Presentation of Self* stretched Simmel's footnote into an entire book, we constantly engage in selective information management in our contacts with others, with an eye towards a desired self-image.[10] Playing a role in this are general social norms or expectations that go together with one's social position as well as more individual notions about how one would like to

9. Simmel, 'Secrecy', op. cit. (note 8), 349.

10. Erving Goffman, *The Presentation of Self in Everyday Life* (London: Penguin Books, 1990).

be seen. Overall, information management complies with the rule that people want to make a good impression, which is also the reason that Goffman speaks of 'impression management'. In carrying out this pursuit, a person selectively reveals information about him or herself and maintains a public self-image in which all individual shortcomings have been rubbed out as much as possible. Personal secrets are the flip side of the picture – Goffman himself speaks of the 'backstage' – the inevitable by-product of this pursuit. The Twittering, e-mailing, text messaging or otherwise digitally networked individual also keeps communicating because of an essentially narcissistic craving for social recognition: Facebook is one gigantic form of 'face-work'.

Information control is impression management is communicative sovereignty. Today's individuals feel like communication sovereigns in front of their PC screens because they have a myriad of information possibilities, addresses and connections to do with as they please. But the core of everyone's communicative sovereignty remains connected with the possibility of withholding information about oneself, just as in the past. Its nature is indeed rather paradoxical because it does not refer to the ability to say more, but to say precisely nothing. This ability to not communicate also defines the ability to communicate: the latter encloses the former, the negation is constitutive for the affirmation. We have a private life in the most literal sense, a life secluded from others, because we can remain silent about ourselves in our dealings with them. Privacy therefore exists in as far as we can be social in an asocial manner, can have personal secrets in public communications. The present ascendancy of sociality over sociability, of indirect over direct communication, changes nothing in that regard.

Confidential

The negation of the ability to communicate about oneself in turn includes a possible negation. Those who harbour personal secrets can also always divulge them in total sovereignty: the privacy of the personal secret exists only thanks to the possibility of its abolition. As a rule, the self-disclosure or confidence creates a bond of trust, a small-scale secret fellowship between intimates who communicate intimately among themselves. Intimate communication is governed by the obligation of confidentiality and discretion. What is told must not be told further (confidentiality, or the requirement of exclusivity); and what is not told must not be questioned further (discretion, or the requirement of reticence). The divulgence of the secret thus does not lift the seal of secrecy on the shared information, but only enlarges the circle of parties to the secret: it turns individual privacy into a socially shared privacy. The medium in which the information is shared makes a difference, however.

In his reflections on the secret, Simmel introduces two elaborations. The first concerns jewellery, which he considers the opposite of the secret. People who wear jewellery want to call attention to themselves: they are not keeping silent about themselves but on the contrary wish to show off their own personality, or a facet of it, to better advantage. The second excursion is about written communication. This is essentially the opposite of the practice of secrecy, as Simmel points out: writing is a medium hostile to secrets, for written intercourse has a public nature that is only potential, to be sure, but also essentially unlimited. 'Writing possesses an objective existence which renounces all guarantees of remaining secret': it is 'likewise wholly unprotected against anybody's taking notice of it.'[11] All mediatized communications are script or text

11. Simmel, 'Secrecy', op. cit. (note 8), 352.

in the broadest sense, communication frozen into 'objective spirit' that in principle can be consulted by third parties. Anyone who in all sincerity puts personal outpourings on paper takes the risk of them being read by eyes for which they were not meant. Besides, textual 'auto-information' is mobile: ego-documents can be passed on to others without the author's permission. The veracity of verbally passed on confidences is always questionable, and they can be dismissed as unreliable gossip; the personal letter, photograph, e-mail, text message or Facebook scribble that is tossed into the public arena, on the other hand, has an objective status: it is an incontestable document.

Post-Authenticity

'It seems as if, with growing cultural expediency, general affairs became ever more public, and individual affairs ever more secret,' stated Simmel back in 1907.[12] He observed the establishment of the

12. Ibid., 336.

modern middle-class culture, which cultivated both the interior of the home and inner life. For the prototypical bourgeois, the territorial interior was the most appropriate hothouse for the growth of the inner psyche. The present-day 'apartment individualism' continues this culture by other means, and as a result its form is changing. Postmodern citizens do not cultivate their inner selves in the living capsule in semi self-seclusion but by sovereignly connecting up with external channels of information. This calls for a follow-up chapter to the story of the 'fall of public man' as the American sociologist Richard Sennett put it in 1977.[13] Sennett's 'public man' is a role player who can effortlessly deal with the difference

13. Richard Sennett, *The Fall of Public Man* (London: Faber and Faber, 1986).

between the social and the individual identity, the acted role and the real self. The 'post-public man', by contrast, always and everywhere strives for as much authenticity as possible. Which is why he or she loathes social masks and has difficulty coping with reticence: communication must be personal and unaffected, sincere and informal. The always-desired point of flight is the confidence, the revelation of a personal secret to clinch the authentic nature of a conversation.

In the name of authentic communication, the personal secret changed during the 1970s from 'inner private property' (Simmel) into a public good. That stage has already passed, although the ethos of authenticity is perhaps the principle heritage of the tumultuous 1960s. In the meanwhile, however, it became completely disassociated from its original utopian overtones and the urge for social change. The ideal of 'daring to speak out' was also gobbled up by the neoliberal spirit of the times: nowadays it is both a democratic right and a civic duty. Communicating transparently became a must for leaders and subordinates, for businesses and governments. 'Express yourself freely. Have the courage of your convictions, your opinions; communicate them, enrich the community, enrich yourself, act, enter into dialogue. Only good can come from the use of your rights provided you respect those of others,' wrote Jean-François Lyotard ironically in an essay in 1990, long before blogging or commenting about news items on media sites became a popular pastime.[14]

14. Jean-Fraçois Lyotard, 'The General Line (for Gilles Deleuze)', in: Jean-François Lyotard, *Political Writings* (London: UCL Press, 1993), 110.

As the ideal of transparent communication became generalized, the disclosure of personal secrets gained a different status. Nowadays, people who present themselves conspicuously in the media, a newsgroup or on Facebook are suspect. The unasked-for public confidence no longer symbolizes sincerity, but cunning. The public confession is seen as a form of attention seeking, a strategy of self-presentation aimed at irritating, shocking, causing a disturbance. Publically coming out with a secret immediately brings with it the suspicion that the revelation is also a concealment, that the divulged information is only a smokescreen for a deeper personal secret of greater importance. Transparency as a screen for intransparency: not just the mass media but all mediatized forms of communication have accustomed us to this paradox. People who surf or e-mail do so in the awareness that they can be duped if private information is voluntarily publicized by others.

Secret Existence

'Since my earliest youth, I have believed that every person in this world has his *no man's land*, where he is his own master. There is the existence that is apparent, and then there is the other existence, unknown to everyone else, that belongs to us without reserve. That is not to say that the one is moral and the other not, or that the one is permissible and the other forbidden. Simply that each person, from time to time, escapes all control, lives in freedom and mastery, alone or with someone else, for an hour a day, or one evening a week, or one day a month. And that this secret and free existence continues from one evening or one day to another, and the hours continue to go on, one after another. Such hours add something to one's visible existence. Unless they have a significance on their own. They can be joy, necessity, or habit, in any case they serve to keep a *general line*,' as the Russian author and Parisian immigrant Nina Berberova has one of her main characters say in *Le roseau revolté*.[15] The 'secret and free existence' to which she alludes clearly is not one of the deeds that must not see the light of day. It is a 'no man's land' because there one discovers something about the self as an unknown, a person without fixed characteristics, a self that no longer is a subject because it no longer finds solid grounds for existence in itself, but only darkness, impersonal thoughts and anonymous-seeming feelings. Nothing about this private existence can be told to others. It defies communication because it leaves one speechless, even though one might, for example, pass the time in no man's land by writing. Its hallmark is the conscious search for the boundary with one's own unconscious, in the admittedly vain hope of making direct contact with this Other. Those who devote themselves to this kind of self-relation do not relinquish secrets of the self, but themselves, and therefore also every claim communicative sovereignty. Every person is also a secret unto themselves, and this is where the personal secret reaches its true limits.

15. Quoted in Lyotard, ibid., 108.

In 1990, the French philosopher Jean-François Lyotard published a short essay dedicated to Gilles Deleuze entitled 'The General Line', in which he provided Berberova's intuitions with a moral-political point. He calls the 'no man's land' in which we give up all claim to self-determination an 'inhuman region' that lies beyond, or beside, the law. This is a secret relation with the self because it is entered into in seclusion, but its private nature goes beyond the right of privacy. The latter raises a legal wall around personal privacy from the idea that every individual subject of the law by definition is the owner of its own self. The kind of self-relation that Berberova refers to, on the contrary, chooses a radical expropriation of this self, its transformation in an anonymous as well as anomic flux of bright ideas, images, affects and other intensities. Yet this privateness is precisely what forms the ultimate legitimization of the right to privacy – even of law in general: legal rules find their ultimate significance in the protection of the privacy that goes beyond every conceivable law. 'The silence of the other inside us' also carries with it an ethical claim, for it wants to be heard. In an environment saturated with information and communication possibilities, this claim is far from evident. 'Now, completely occupied with the legitimacy of exchanges with others in the community, we are inclined to neglect our duty to listen to this other; we are inclined to negate the second existence it requires of us,' according to Lyotard.[16] There is nothing to add to this conclusion: it has only become more pertinent since 1990.

16. Ibid., 111.

Maurizio
Lazzarato

'Pastoral Power'

Beyond Public

and Private

The Italian-
French sociologist
Maurizio Lazzarato
uses Foucault's
concept of 'pastoral
power' to analyse
the demise of the
separation between
public and private
space. Furthermore,
his study of the

social policies
concerning unem-
ployment shows
how 'the produc-
tion of guilt' is
more and more
often being used as
a strategy; a process
already described
by Franz Kafka in
his literature.

There are different ways to approach the issue of the public and the private. I would like to do so on the basis of research that I am conducting into precariousness. The state, in its government of the poor, the unemployed and the clients of social services, is demolishing the separation between public space and private space and between public life and private life as its interventions in the life of individuals, in what is their most 'intimate', most subjective, most singular sphere, have become more and more systematic.

In the first part I will analyse Michel Foucault's concept of pastoral power, as it can help us understand how techniques of power are used to guide the conduct of the governed and how they affect the lives of individuals beyond the separation of the public and the private. In the second part I will use a playful 'scherzo' to consider the work of Kafka, which demonstrates how the administration crosses the line between public and private through its actions and how this affects the individual and invades his life. Both parts are informed by the experiences of my research into precariousness.

The labour market is a place where different facilities operate and heterogeneous power relations exist. Besides the general and universal laws enacted by parliament that, for example, define legal working hours, besides the regulations and norms negotiated by social partners – employer's organizations and trade unions – that concern collective labour agreements as well as the modalities for unemployment funding and benefits of the French centre for work and income (Association pour l'emploi dans le commerce et l'industrie or Assedic) there is an 'archipelago' of actual power relations that is neither global nor general, but local, molecular and singular.

The individual monitoring of the unemployed, the techniques for reinsertion of the 'RMIstes',[1] enterprise management, the coaching of both workers and unemployed, the generalized continuous training, the facilities for access to credit and debt settlement, and so forth, introduce processes of subjection that are different from the submission to a law, a contract or a democratic institution.

1. A person who has no job or unemployment benefits and who receives a monthly revenue of approximately 400 euros from the state.

These techniques of molecular differentiation, individualization and submission, outlined or prefigured by what Michel Foucault calls 'pastoral power', have been adjusted, modified, improved and upgraded, first in the seventeenth and eighteenth centuries by the 'police' of the *raison d'état*, and then at the end of the nineteenth and the beginning of the twentieth centuries by the welfare state (whose French name, *état providence*, is reminiscent of its religious origins), thus transforming techniques for the 'government of souls' into techniques for the 'political government of men'. This genealogy allows us to specify the molecular nature of the power effects of liberal governmentality. It also allows us to understand how the government of life beyond the divide between public and private functions. For 'pastoral power' or 'biopolitics', 'privacy' or 'private life' never existed, except for the rich. The only actual private thing in modernity is private property.

Christianity, the only religion that organized itself as a church, 'has given rise to an art of conducting, directing, leading, guiding, taking in hand, and manipulating men, an art of monitoring them and urging them on step by step, an art with the function of taking charge of men collectively and individually throughout their life and at every moment of their existence.'[2]

This art of government is completely unknown in political philosophy and in the theories of law. This form of power, the 'strangest form of power, the form of power that is most typical of the West, and that will also have the greatest and most durable fortune', which is 'unique . . . in the entire history of civilizations',[3] has no relationship with the Greek and Roman political tradition, unlike the majority of modern and contemporary political models.[4]

Pastoral power and its modern avatars must not be confused with the procedures used to submit men to a law, a

2. Michel Foucault, *Security, Territory, Population: Lectures at the Collège de France, 1977-78*, translated by G. Burchell (Basingstoke and New York: Palgrave Macmillan, 2007), 165.

3. Ibid., 173.

4. Foucault would have been doubly astonished by Giogio Agamben's interpretation of biopolitics. First because his theory of power is presented as a metaphysics and second because he situates his genealogy within the Roman political tradition. This is categorically rejected by Foucault.

sovereign or to democratic institutions. Governing, says Foucault, is not the same as 'reigning or ruling', it is not the same thing as 'commanding' or even 'laying down the law'. It encompasses all the theories and practices of sovereignty (of the king, the prince, the people), the theories and practices of the *arkhè*, in other words, it is a political organization that is based on the question of knowing who is entitled to command and who is entitled to obey (the basis of the analysis of the political by Hannah Arendt and Jacques Rancière), all those juridico-democratic theories and practices, including most of the currents in Marxism that neglect governmental procedures of conduct although they constitute the essence of power relations in capitalism, especially in contemporary capitalism.

Michel Foucault sums up the characteristics of this 'micropower' by stressing what distinguishes each of them from the modern and antique practices and theories of 'macropower'. Pastoral power establishes a series of complex, continual and paradoxical relationships between men. These relationships are not political in the way that democratic institutions, political philosophy and almost all revolutionary and critical theories understand it. Pastoral power is 'a strange technology of power treating the vast majority of men as a flock with a few as shepherds'.[5]

Contrary to sovereignty, it is

5. Michel Foucault, 'Omnes et singulatim', in: *Politics, Philosophy, Culture: Interviews and Other Writings 1977-1984*, edited by Lawrence D. Kritzman (New York: Routledge, 1988), 63.

not exercised over a territory (city, kingdom, principality or republic), but over a 'multiplicity in movement' (a flock for the practices of the church and a 'population' for the governmentality).[6] Instead of touching individuals as legal subjects 'capable of voluntary actions', capable of transferring right and delegating their power to representatives, capable of assuming the magistracies of the *polis*, pastoral power is aimed at 'living subjects', their daily behaviour, their subjectivity and their conscience.

6. The space in which pastoral power is exercised is not of the same nature as that of sovereignty and of discipline. Whereas sovereignty 'capitalizes a territory' and discipline is exerted in a closed space through a hierarchic and functional distribution of elements, pastoral power, like the police at first and the welfare state later, is exercised over a multiplicity in motion and on its 'environment'. Pastoral power, transformed from a government of souls into political government of men, will 'try to plan a milieu in terms of events or series of events or possible elements, of series that will have to be regulated within a multivalent and transformable framework'. Foucault, *Security, Territory, Population*, op. cit. (note 2), 34.

The shepherd, Foucault points out, is essentially not a judge or a man of the law or a citizen, but a doctor. Pastoral power is a 'wholesome' power, it takes care of both the flock and each member of the flock. Contrary to sovereignty (or the law) which is exercised collectively, pastoral power is exercised in a 'distributive' manner (its action is deployed 'from individual to individual', step by step, and it is communicated by singularities). It deals with each soul, each situation and its particulars, rather than with the unity that is formed by the whole.

Its action is local and infinitesimal rather than global and general.[7]

Pastoral power, like its successor, the 'police'[8] of the *raison d'état* and the welfare state, deals with details, intervenes in the infinitesimal, in the molecular of a situation and a subjectivity. It is a continuous, permanent power. It is not exercised intermittently, like the power that is grounded in law, sovereignty or citizenship (transfer of rights by contract, delegation of power by vote, exercise of magisterial power, and so forth), but all day long during one's entire life.

Pastoral power is individualizing. The techniques of pastoral individualization are not based on status of birth or wealth, but on a 'subtle economy' that combines merits and faults, their trajectory and their circuits.[9] This economy of souls establishes an overall dependency, a relationship of absolute and unconditional submission and obedience, not to laws or 'reasoned' principles, but to the will of another individual. 'Obey

7. The political government of men is not primarily aimed at 'the common good'. In the eighteenth century, government was already defined as a way of arranging and conducting men and things, not as a collective whole, for the 'common good' (kingdom, city, republic, democracy) but for 'convenient ends'. This implies a plurality of particular ends (producing the greatest amount of riches, population growth, and so forth); their convergence, coordination and synthesis, however, are problematic.

8. Policing consists of furthering both the life of the citizens and the strength of the state. 'In seeing to health and supplies, it deals with the preservation of life; concerning trade, factories, workers, the poor and public order, it deals with the conveniences of life. In seeing to the theatre, literature, entertainment, its object is life's pleasures.' Foucault, *Politics, Philosophy, Culture*, op. cit. (note 5), 81.

9. The shepherd continually manages this economy of merits 'that presupposes an analysis into precise elements, mechanisms of transfer, procedures of reversal, and of the interplay of support between conflicting elements between the shepherd and the believer'. Foucault, *Security, Territory, Population*, op. cit. (note 2), 228.

because it is absurd' is the motto of Christian submission, whose rules of monastic life constitute the end, while the Greek citizen only allowed himself to be led by law en by the rhetoric of man, so that, according to Foucault, 'the general category of obedience' was unknown to the Greeks.

The shepherd is also a doctor of the soul, who teaches modes of existence. The shepherd must not confine himself to teaching the truth, he must also first and foremost guide consciences by taking 'non-global and non-general', specific and singular action. Thus Saint Gregory names up to 36 different ways of teaching, according to the individuals one addresses (rich, poor, married, sick, merry or sad, and so forth). Teaching does not pass through the enunciation of general principles, but through 'an observation, a supervision, a direction exercised at every moment and with the least discontinuity possible over the sheep's whole, total conduct'. Pastoral knowledge thus produces a 'never-ending knowledge of the behaviour and conduct of the members of the flock he supervises'.[10]

10. Ibid., 235.

The techniques of admission, examination of conscience, confession, and so forth, are all instruments with which to examine and investigate the relationship to the self and the relationship with others, instruments that influence the affects and sensibility of each subjectivity. The shepherd 'will have to account for every act of each of his sheep, for everything that may have happened between them, and everything good and evil they may have done at any time'.[11]

11. Ibid., 226.

The final aim of spiritual direction by pastoral power is not self-mastery, autonomy and liberty, as in ancient society, but on the contrary, the renouncement of the will, humility, and the neutralization of all individual, personal and egoistic activities. Pastoral power is also not a power that establishes and constitutes a community of equals and peers that is guided by the principles of equality and liberty. It neither favours nor promotes citizens acting according to the modalities of the republican and democratic tradition, but rather is a system of generalized mutual dependencies. The techniques of pastoral power aim at the fabrication of a subject who is 'subjected' to networks that imply the general servitude of one to all.

The assimilation and transformation of these techniques of individualization by the police of the *raison d'état* in the sixteenth and seventeenth centuries did not fundamentally change its nature. The police assures a 'a set of controls, decisions, and constraints brought to bear on men themselves, not insofar as they have a status or are something in the order, hierarchy, and social structure, but insofar as they do something, are able to do it, and undertake to do it throughout their life.'[12]

12. Ibid., 419.

Today the economy of merits and faults, the direction of everyday conduct and subjection are still the motor of practices and discourses that are deemed to individualize, control, regulate and order the behaviour of those that are governed in work, schooling, health, consumption and communication, and so forth.

The management techniques that extend from the enterprise to 'social security' (the individualizing regulation of 'the unemployed, the RMIstes, the poor') and to society in general (school, hospital, communication, consumption) are always inspired by those molecular practices of distribution of merits and faults, the production of dependency and subjection, even when dependency and subjection are achieved, as in the case of the employer, by activating and mobilizing the individual's initiative and liberty or power to act.

Pastoral power is not exercised in the light, transparency and visibility of public space, but in the opacity of the 'private' relationship (between individuals, between institution and individual), in the dark everyday life of factories, schools, hospitals and social services. This molecular model of power relations, which produces multiple fractal divisions and hierarchies that are more subtle and more mobile than those of traditional oligarchies of wealth and birth, will continue to expand and grow exponentially under capitalism.

Individual Monitoring of the Unemployed and the RMIstes as a Technique for Pastoral Control

I will now quote a few short extracts from interviews that we are conducting with RMIstes and that touch on the 'individual monitoring' (a monthly interview) to which they are subjected by the institutions for the control of the poor.

The relationships that are established within the framework of individual monitoring between officials and clients consist of the action (of the agent) on the activity (of the client), with which the former is trying to bring structure to the possibilities for action of the latter. So it constitutes a 'strategic' relationship between two subjects in the sense that, although it remains asymmetrical, both official and client are 'free'. As Foucault would say, in other words, they can act differently. This is expressed in techniques that are aimed at guiding the conduct of the clients, controlling their behaviour and making them enter a pre-established trajectory (project is the word that is most often used) and identity. The techniques that are used in individual monitoring touch on life, intimacy and the most subjective aspects of the clients of the RMI. They induce the 'poor' to question themselves, their 'lifestyle' and their projects. They force them to work on themselves. In applying these techniques, the state and its institutions cross the boundaries between public space and private space, between public life and private life on a daily basis The state and its institutions invade the private life of individuals, act on subjectivity, mobilize the most 'intimate' forces, direct behaviour and use interventions (controls) that overstep the limits of the home to enter into private space and initiate 'trials'.

D.: *Skill assessments, for example, they're offering them to you all the time and even if you know what they are, there's always some aspect that touches on the intimate. I know people who have undergone in-depth skill assessments and in spite of the fact that they are aimed at finding a job, they are also an exercise that not everybody can cope with, that you aren't necessarily used to, a kind of assessment of your life in which you ask yourself questions, you think about yourself, it's a kind of intrusion using some horrible vocabulary that still forces you to look at yourself.*

F.: *Because I look a little young, and I was young, actually, the relationship that you get often takes on the shape of a relationship between adult and adolescent – and in my case it was a woman as well – I will eventually find my way, she's just there to give me advice, at the moment it isn't really worrying that I don't have a steady job . . . Sometimes it's just easier to play along, to tell them what they want to hear instead of being 'really sincere'.*

In 'individual monitoring' you are held to account. Once every month the clients have to talk about themselves (or play-act), they have to tell what they are doing with their life and their time.

T.: *I for one was always in a panic at the end of the month: are they going to strike me from the RMI, how I am going to pay my rent this month . . . Often I would say to myself: Is it really worth the bother? Why don't I find a part-time job that will pay just as much but where there won't be a million people coming to hassle me about accounting for myself? . . . You don't know what they're like, those people from the CAF . . . Every time you go, you feel like you're back at school, you're a little kid and they ask 'Have you been behaving?' and 'Are you doing the right things?' And you sit there and you say: 'Jesus, all this just so they will give me those measly 300 euros.'*

But individual monitoring also brings out techniques and strategies of resistance against the institutional invasion of 'privacy'. Techniques for resisting government, techniques for governing the self and regaining mastery over one's life.

The production of what economists call 'human capital' or, in other words, an 'autonomous' individual who is 'responsible' for his employability, who makes an effort and sets out projects in order to find a job, passes through interventions in the life, desires, passions, opinions and choices of the individual. Liberal rhetoric would have us believe that desires, opinions and choices constitute the private domain where the sovereign individual can act freely. In reality, however, they are the object of increasingly violent public action as unemployment rises and incrusts itself in society as a structural reality.

D.: Once she asked me questions about what I was interested in and what I wanted to do with my life and why I had chosen to do what I had done and I returned the question: 'And why are you working with the social services?' Because I thought, this is overstepping the line and I didn't have to tell her everything about my life . . . I think that she insisted because it had to do with the idea she had of me, with her inter-pretation of the situation; that I was someone who hadn't yet found his calling or his way and that he has to be helped to understand what is happening to him because I have skills but I just have to get on the right track.

U.: I couldn't bear this type of rela-tionship where I had to justify myself and tell my life story, so I told her absolutely nothing – she must have thought I was some kind of nut job.

L.: The counsellor asked me to talk about what I did all day, well, I told her: I ask myself questions about fidelity, it is part of my work. She says to me: I don't see the connection. But, in my view, you just can't answer that question, what do you do all day? Because when you start answering that question, you are justifying your-self, you're accounting for yourself. You shouldn't have to do that for 400 euros.

But even if they want to resist such an intrusion into their private lives, such violence perpetrated against the person and his subjectivity, the clients are still perturbed by the 'work on the self' to which they are compelled by the institutions. They start asking themselves questions because the 'interview' and the questions of the counsellor work on and find their way into the client's subjectivity, in spite of themselves and in spite of their will to resist invasion by governmental action.

E.: I play along even when sometimes it touches on things that upset me, like for example being confronted with starting projects that are conceivable for me and realistic in this context. Sometimes it brings me to the ques-tion: What is it that makes you get up in the morning and do things? This type of monitoring also forces you to think about 'projects' that you would like to work on but haven't started yet – or will never start – because you don't know, because it's hard and it makes you ask yourself questions about what you're up to, about what your life is and 'which projects' – because this word keeps popping up – you are working on. But they don't get it, in the sense that it could affect me when they use those words. It's as if we were not talking about the same thing, but with the same words.

Institutions are not satisfied with entering into the intimate sphere of a person, they don't limit themselves to conducting the client's conduct through 'individual monitoring', mapping out his life, forcing him to work on his self and accessing his innermost subjectivity. They physically enter the 'private lives' of individuals, or in other words, the incitements and prescriptions of monitoring can take place in that most private of spaces, the home. Through their counsellors, state institutions invite themselves into the home to make inquiries and question the 'private lives' of clients, applying two types of control: home visits and neighbourhood inquiries. In the first case, an agent focuses on the client, enters into the apartment or the house, inspects the rooms, the bathroom, asks to see electricity, telephone and rent bills, asks questions about living arrangements and specifically verifies if the client is living alone. Because if he is living with someone, this person could be supporting him and his benefits could be cut.

I once was present at such a visit, because one of the techniques you can use to defend yourself against this unbearable invasion of private life is to receive the controller with a group of people. The presence of someone in your apartment or home who is keeping tabs on your 'life' and checks with whom and how you live is an exceptionally violent form of intrusion.

The state, through its officials, invites itself into the private lives of individuals and even inquires about their love life. The following exchange with RMIste artists (visual artists, composers, filmmakers), recorded in one of our research localities, clearly demonstrates how the state shamelessly intervenes in what liberal and even state ideologies consider to be the most private aspect of the life of individuals: in their love relationships.

About the rent . . . something you might call 'the RMI and love' [laughter]. At a certain moment we, my ex-girlfriend and I, decided to rent an apartment. I knew I was entitled to benefits from the RMI. And I filled in a simulation form on the site of the CAF (the institution that decides on the allocation of the RMI) by checking the RMI. And the simulation form answered: Yes, you are entitled to benefits from 300 to 400 euros a month. Knowing that my girlfriend was making a good living and that I was earning whatever I was earning. But she didn't support me, I paid for my own food, we agreed that I would pay a small part of the rent, according to what I earned. We lived as a couple, but for the rest . . . In short, we finally were able to sign the lease because she could put down a great deposit. But in the end, the CAF would not grant me the benefits, because they considered us to be a single household and they look at the incomes of both partners. In fact, from the moment we registered at the same address, they said 'you're a couple, so we look at the couple's income'.

M.: You didn't get it for how long?

To.: *During the two years we lived together, and immediately after we separated, I got it back.*

S.: *It's like a premium on divorce.*

To.: *In the letter I wrote to the CAF, I said: I know that the CAF isn't there to play Cupid, but still . . . [laughter]*

P.: *So the RMIstes should only associate with RMIstes if they want to get support. It's the Indian system, the caste system: the rich with the rich, the poor with the poor [laughter].*

What interests me most in the following excerpt from an article on home visits[13] in which 'the RMI and love' still plays a role is a remark that was made almost in passing. The consultation between controller[14] and controlled is 'like a trial' (anticipating the final part on Kafka), but a very strange trial, because it takes place within the walls of the home of the accused, the suspect, who is 'guilty' of cohabitation (he failed to report that he

13. Vincent Dubois, 'Le paradoxe du contrôleur. Incertitude et contrainte institutionnelle dans le contrôle des assistés sociaux', *Actes de la recherche en sciences socials*, vol. 3 (2009) no. 178.

14. There are different control techniques: 'Me, I have my own personal working method. For example, I give the client the impression that I am going nowhere. But actually my interview is pre-established. So I talk about his situation and his work and then I say "sorry, I forgot something". But in fact, I'm trying to rattle him or her. Or I close my briefcase and pretend to leave and then come back to ask the question that I'd supposedly forgotten, but that I had in the back of my mind from the start. Well, then I try to rattle him a bit because some of them are prepared. There are already three controls in the file, so they know the drill. I try to . . . throw them off a bit, because some of them even prepare what they're going to say, they've been briefed by a social worker.' Ibid.

is living with someone who might be able to support him).

There are only two chairs. So he remains standing in front of us on the other side of the table, so that the whole scene takes on the aspect of a trial, especially because he talks a lot to explain and clarify his situation. He is visibly tense, his voice is rather shaky. The controller asks for a number of documents and identity papers. Somewhat abruptly and with a natural air he asks about the nature of the housing situation. The client immediately answers: 'Yeah, we're living together.' The rest of the meeting regards the qualification of that situation.

The man: Cohabitation, I have no idea . . . We have separate accounts, we pay for things separately. I came to live here because I didn't have a place to stay, but I didn't see myself as . . . In the beginning, for me, it was temporary. You mustn't get the idea that we were trying to cheat.

The controller: No, if they send a controller, it's to look at the situation, not because we think you've been cheating. We look at the facts. So here, in the beginning this was temporary, and now it's a temporary arrangement that is lasting . . . [The controller asks for the date that they started living together].

The man, after a few moments of silence: And do you take this into account in your calculation of the benefits?

The controller: Yes.

The second type of state control consists of talking to the neighbours and asking them if the client really lives alone en what his lifestyle is. If he turns out to be a single parent, the neighbours are asked if he is really single, and so forth. . . . The institutions for the control of the poor train the controllers to answer criticisms and eventual complaints by clients. Here we have a 'list of arguments' intended for the senior staff that trains the controllers. It attempts to prepare for any objections, refusals and criticisms that the clients might express during visits. A few words of advice to the controllers:

When 'methods of control on location are put into question'
Answer: The control that you mention, which we call 'on location', is only one control method among many that we use in certain cases. Among the 6 million clients whom we control each year, we only use it in 10 per cent of all cases.

In the case of a critical remark like 'incursion into the private home, neighbourhood inquiry = grassing' you must answer: if the controllers have reason to visit the home of the client or to conduct a neighbour-hood inquiry, it is in fact because they cannot base the conclusion of their inquiry on a single element (the opinion of a neighbour or the 'word' of a client).

Every day television and radio enter your home, blurring the bounda-ries between private and public and redefining the limits of both public and private space. But these are still external devices that you can 'easily avoid'. Physical intrusion into private space deeply destabilizes individuals by humiliating them.

The new French legislation (2009) that has replaced the RMI is even more invasive. Not only do you have to disclose your actual resources (if you have had a job or if you have an income), but also your bank balance, whether you have life insur-ance, whether you bought shares when you had a job, whether you are a house owner, whether your parents or friends can help you, and so forth. The state conducts an actual inquiry into your 'lifestyle'. The client must be completely transparent[15] to the logic of the institution.

15. 'Transparant', but not in the figurative sense. Undressing is not a metaphor. A controller: 'Some of them will say to me: [with a whining voice] "Oh, I'm sick . . ." Then they start undressing, they show me their scars. Then I say with a friendly voice: "No, no, you can put your clothes back on, I'm not a doctor." Some say they're sick, they hope that I will not ask too many ques-tions or ask them for their papers. Some say: "Oh dear I don't know where my head is, you see, you mustn't ask me too many questions, I've been ill," or "I've got cancer." That's the thing I fear the most. Each time I tell them: "Listen, I'm very sorry, but . . ."' Ibid.

Now I would like to quote a few short extracts from a round table discussion that we have held with agents of the unemployment insurance programme and of the management of the RMI who intervene in the monitoring and control of the unemployed and the poor. These extracts will serve as an introduction to the last part which bears on the production of responsi-bility and guilt with the recipients of unemployment insurance and of the RMI.

M.: *In my work, what the logic of reinsertion teaches me, contrary to the logic of integration, is to act on the person. In other words, it's the person who must qualify himself and enter into a process in order to raise his level. And that's the real problem with structural unemployment, because you have to put the responsibility with the individuals: they are the ones who aren't capable of finding a job and in that case social work consists of acting directly on the person. And when the work of the ANPE connects with the work of the external educator, it is within this logic. It defines our practices: we already think in advance that the persons themselves have to increase their skills.*

A.: *At Pôle emploi, the employment and benefits agency, that is what we propagate, we make the 'client' responsible for his situation. That is it, really. And in the face of what happens, it's the generalization of a badly assumed or completely assumed feeling of complicity and the managing of a form of everyday powerlessness that breeds resistances, but managed on an individual level. Because the counsellor at the other side of the table is also held responsible for his capacity or incapacity in making the 'client' employable.*

Kafka, the Production of Guilt and the Blurring of the Division between Public and Private

'The Workmen's Accident Insurance Institution . . . is a creation of the labour movement. It should therefore be filled with the radiant spirit of progress. But what happens? The institution is a dark nest of bureaucrats, in which I function as the solitary display-Jew.'

The production of guilt is a strategic action of neoliberalism that can also be analysed through Kafka's work. Kafka was very much ahead of his time, for his characters speak about a reality, a form of labour organization and public administration (the welfare state) and a life that seems closer to our times than that of the interbellum.

Bürgel, the 'connecting' secretary in *The Castle*, says something that sounds familiar to us: 'In that respect we don't acknowledge any distinction between ordinary time and work time. Such distinctions are alien to us.' And K., the land surveyor in *The Castle*, experiences a power relation that could be qualified, on the basis of Foucault's terms, as biopolitical, in the sense that it implicates life as a whole, beyond the separation of 'public life' and 'private life': 'Nowhere else had K. ever seen one's official position and one's life so intertwined as they were here, so intertwined that it sometimes seemed as though office and life had switched places.'

Official administration institutions like the RMI, unemployment insurance, and so forth, already announce something before they articulate a discourse, whatever it may be. They announce that there is a social problem (unemployment, employability, and so forth) but it is not society that the institution calls on to insure the individual follow-up, it is you, 'Joseph K.!' There is a shift from 'there is a social problem' to 'you are the problem!' This shift is enclosed in the institution itself, in its practices and its procedures, before it enters the minds of social workers and clients.

Like in *The Trial*, the accusation is never clearly formulated: it is never clearly stated that 'being unemployed is your own fault', for that would lead to resistance on the part of the client. As for the fault of unemployment, it has unclear, undefined and imprecise boundaries. But very soon you forget that the accusation is more than vague. Slowly it installs doubt into the mind of the client, there is a growing feeling that we are guilty of something, that we are at fault, because we have received a document, we have been summoned and must present ourselves at that address on that day at that time in that office. Joseph K.'s arrest does not really change his life, he continues to go to work and to live as before. He is thus both under arrest and free. Whether you're guilty or innocent, 'We're opening a file on you, Joseph K.!'

Somewhere there is a file with officials who are working on it, but all you will ever see are the flunkeys, never the main procurators. On the other hand, is there really a vertical organization of offices, with chiefs and subordinates, or does everything happen in a horizontal manner, between subalterns? Rather both at the same time, but anyway, the right information is always to be found in the next office, you always have to knock on the next door, and so on. Are the offices of the administration still part of 'public' space or have they been installed in our 'private' space?

The number 3949 is a telephone platform for the unemployed and the poor that replaces face-to-face meetings with institution agents. It is the contemporary version of the office that is no longer situated in either private or public space. The number 3949 must be dialled repeatedly before you fall on different officials and verify if the same law is being applied because everyone has his own interpretation of it. Often the officials don't even know about it, and anyway, they hang up after six minutes. You then have to knock on the next door, and so on. The number 3949 is the deterritorialization of the office and the official.

Like the accusation, the 'tribunals' in *The Trial* have no clearly defined limits ('You shouldn't imagine these barriers as a fixed boundary,' says Barnabas in *The Castle*). They are spread out over the city and no-one really knows what they are made up of. There is no clearly established distinction between public space and private space, the two continually overlap and form a continuity that leaves no room for 'private life'.

I find that Kafka's law is more in keeping with social law and social security regulations, and so forth, than with penal law: social security laws are relatively malleable, continually proliferating and permanently expanding. Of the three types of acquittal, actual acquittal (no-one can influence it), apparent acquittal (demands a concentrated effort over a limited period) and protraction of the proceedings (demands a more modest but interminable effort), it is the latter that concerns us most. Actual acquittal exists only theoretically. Apparent acquittal is derived from disciplinary societies in which you go from one internment to the next and from one guilt to the other: from the family to school, from school to the army, from the army to the factory, and so forth. And each passage is marked by a judgement or an evaluation. You go from one acquittal: you are no longer a child, you are no longer a pupil, and so forth, to the next trial and another file: you are a soldier, you are a worker, you are a pensioner, and so forth.

Unlimited protraction, however, maintains the trial in its first phase for an indeterminable period, in other words, in a situation where you are dependent on the presumption of innocence and guilt (you are on trial: you have been summoned and you have a file). In unlimited protraction, the sentence of guilty or innocent never comes. The state of suspension between innocence and guilt forces you to be mobilized, disposable and on your toes at all times.

Unlimited protraction demands even greater attention, 'a more modest but interminable effort,' says the painter Titorelli or, in other words, a greater subjective involvement. The law has no interiority, the law is empty (the law is pure form), for it is you, 'Joseph K.', who, if all goes well, must contribute to its construction and to the construction of your sentence by working on your file and your summons.

The monitoring relationship that is woven on a framework of guilt is a trial in which you have to play along while withdrawing at the same time. You have to anticipate developments, twists and turns and bumps in the road, even if you do not really believe in them (cynicism of both officials and clients). Anyway, your subjectivity is summoned and becomes implicated. It works, thinks, hesitates and questions itself, even against your better judgement. The indefinite prolongation of the first phase in the trial also requires endless monitoring that goes beyond the boundaries of public and private. The timetable of the accused and that of the monitoring are adjusted to one another.

'The interrogations, for instance, they're only very short, if you ever don't have the time or don't feel like going to them you can offer an excuse, with some judges you can even arrange the injunctions together a long time in advance, in essence all it means is that, as the accused, you have to report to the judge from time to time.'

Like in *The Trial*, being accused is no walk in the park. It is work, you have to keep an eye on your file, spend a lot of time on it (the industrial spends all his time and money on his defence).

You have to stay abreast of the development of the law and its changes and be aware of its subtleties. You have to hoist yourself to the same level of knowledge as the officials and even surpass them. The RMIstes prepare their meetings, their confrontations with the institution by elaborating certain tactics. They refine 'projects' that are more or less fictional. They all operate by directly or indirectly supplying clues and information, they all function on the feedback from the institution.

In disciplinary societies, penal law was legitimized by the battle against illegalisms (transgressions of the law) and by social peace, but in reality, instead of eliminating these illegalisms, it has in turn produced and differentiated crimes and criminals. Similarly, social law in societies of control has been legitimized by the struggle against unemployment and for full employment, but all it has done is invent, multiply and differentiate countless ways of not working full-time. Social law, like penal law, has not failed, but fully succeeded. It has constructed a new dimension in which the distinction between private and public no longer exists.

Daniel J. Solove

The Meaning and Value of Privacy

Appeal for a Pluralistic Definition of the Concept of Privacy

According to Daniel Solove, professor of law at Washington University Law School, we need to reconsider the concept of privacy. He appeals for a more pluralistic reading of the concept, to facilitate the recognition of problems pertaining to privacy. In his most recent publication *Understanding Privacy*,[1] he has developed a framework for this. In the following article he discusses the ideas unfolded in the book.

1. Daniel J. Solove, *Understanding Privacy* (Cambridge, MA: Harvard University Press, 2008). More information about this book can be found online at: understanding-privacy.com.

Our privacy is under assault. Businesses are collecting an unprecedented amount of personal data, recording the items we buy at the supermarket, the books we buy online, our web surfing activity, our financial transactions, the movies we watch, the videos we rent, and much more. Nearly every organization and company we interact with now has tons of personal data about us. Companies we've never heard of also possess profiles of us. Digital dossiers about our lives and personalities are being assembled in distant databases, and they are being meticulously studied and analysed to make judgments about us: What products are we likely to buy? Are we a good credit risk? What price would we be willing to pay for certain items? How good of a customer are we? Are we likely to be cooperative and not likely to return items or complain or call customer service?

Today, government has an unprecedented hunger for personal data. It is tapping into the data possessed by businesses and other organizations, including libraries. Many businesses readily comply with government requests for data. Government agencies are mining this personal data, trying to determine whether a person might likely engage in criminal or terrorist activity in the future based on patterns of behaviour, purchases and interests.[2] If a government computer decides that you are a likely threat, then you might find yourself on a watch list, you might have

2. Robert O'Harrow, *No Place to Hide* (New York: Free Press, 2005)

difficulty flying, and there might be further negative consequences in the future.

The threat to privacy involves more than just records. Surveillance cameras are popping up everywhere. It is getting increasingly harder to have an unrecorded moment in public. In the USA, the National Security Agency is engaging in massive telephone surveillance. In the UK, millions of CCTV cameras monitor nearly every nook and cranny of public space.[3] At work, many employers monitor nearly everything – every call their

3. Jeffrey Rosen, *The Naked Crowd: Reclaiming Security and Freedom in an Anxious Age* (New York: Random House, 2004).

employees make, every keystroke they type, every website they visit.

Beyond the government and businesses, we're increasingly invading each other's privacy – and exposing our own personal information. The generation of young people growing up today are using blogs and social network websites at an unprecedented rate, spilling intimate details about their personal lives online that are available for anybody anywhere in the world to read.[4] The gossip that circulates in high school and college is no longer ephemeral and

4. Daniel J. Solove, *The Future of Reputation: Gossip, Rumor, and Privacy on the Internet* (New Haven: Yale University Press, 2007).

fleeting – it is now permanently available on the Internet, and it can readily be accessed by doing a Google search under a person's name.

With all these developments, many are asking whether privacy is still alive. With so much information being gathered, with so much surveillance, with so much disclosure, how can people expect privacy anymore? If we can't expect privacy, is it possible to protect it? Many contend that fighting for privacy is a losing battle, so we might as well just grin and bear it.

Do People Expect Privacy Anymore?

These attitudes, however, represent a failure to understand what privacy is all about. The law often focuses on whether we expect privacy or not – and it refuses to protect privacy in situations where we don't expect it. But expectations are the wrong thing to look at. The law isn't merely about preserving the existing state of affairs – it is about shaping the future. The law should protect privacy not because we expect it, but because we desire it.

Privacy is often understood narrowly, and these restrictive concepts lead to people neglecting to recognize privacy harms. For example, it may be true that many businesses hold a lot of personal data about you. Does this mean you lack a privacy interest in that data? Those who view privacy narrowly as keeping information totally secret might say that you no longer have privacy in information that others possess.

But privacy is about much more than keeping secrets. It is also about confidentiality – data can be known by others, yet we have social norms about maintaining that information in confidence. For example, although librarians know information about the books we read, they understand

that they have an obligation to keep the information confidential. Doctors know our medical information, but they, too, are under a duty of confidentiality.

Privacy also involves maintaining data security. Those who possess data should have an obligation to keep it secure and out of the hands of identity thieves and fraudsters. They should have an obligation to prevent data leaks.

Another dimension of privacy is having control over our information. Just because companies and the government have data about you doesn't mean that they should be allowed to use it however they desire. We can readily agree that they shouldn't be able to use personal information to engage in discrimination. The law can and should impose many other limits on the kinds of decisions that can be made using personal data.

Those that use data about us should have the responsibility of notifying us about the data they have and how they plan to use it. People should have some say in how their information is used. There needs to be better 'data due process'. Currently, innocent people are finding themselves on terrorist watch lists and with no recourse to challenge their inclusion on the list. Financial and employment decisions are made about people based on profiles and information they don't even know exist.

Privacy thus involves more than keeping secrets – it is about how we regulate information flow, how we ensure that others use our information responsibly, how we exercise control over our information, how we should limit the way others can use our data.

Some argue that it is impossible for the law to limit how others use our data, but this is false. Copyright law is a clear example of the law regulating the way information is used and providing control over that data. I'm not suggesting that copyright law is the answer to privacy, but it illustrates that it is possible for the law to restrict uses of data if it wants to.

We can protect privacy, even in light of all the collection, dissemination and use of our information. And it is something we must do if we want to protect our freedom and intellectual activity in the future. But how? The first steps involve rethinking the concept and value of privacy.

Rethinking the Concept of Privacy

Privacy is a concept in disarray. Commentators have lamented that the concept of privacy is so vague that it is practically useless. When we speak of privacy invasions, we often fail to clearly explain why such an infringement is harmful. The interests on the other side – free speech, efficient consumer transactions, and security – are often much more readily comprehended. The result is that privacy frequently loses in the balance. Even worse, courts and policymakers often fail to recognize privacy interests at all.

Many attempts to conceptualize privacy do so by attempting to locate the common denominator for all things we view as private. This method of conceptualizing privacy, however, faces a difficult dilemma. If we choose a common denominator that is broad enough to encompass nearly everything, then the conception risks the danger of being over-inclusive or too vague. If we choose a narrower common denominator, then the risk is that the conception is too restrictive.

There is a way out of this dilemma: We can conceptualize privacy in a different way. The philosopher Ludwig Wittgenstein argued that some concepts are best understood as family resemblances – they include things that 'are *related* to one another in many different ways'.[5] Some things share a network of similarities without one particular thing in common. They are related in the way family members are related. You might have your mother's eyes, your brother's hair, your sister's nose – but you all might not have one common feature. There is no common denominator. Nevertheless, you bear a resemblance to each other.[6] We should understand privacy in this way. Privacy is not one thing, but a plurality of many distinct yet related things.

5. Ludwig Wittgenstein, *Philosophical Investigations*, translated by G.E.M. Anscombe (Oxford: Blackwell, 2001 [1953]), § 65.

6. As Wittgenstein observes, instead of being related by a common denominator, some things share 'a complicated network of similarities overlapping and criss-crossing: sometimes overall similarities, sometimes similarities of detail'. Ibid., § 66.

One of the key issues in developing a theory of privacy is how to deal with the variability of attitudes and beliefs about privacy. Privacy is a product of norms, activities, and legal protections. As a result, it is culturally and historically contingent. For example, it is widely accepted today that the naked body is private in the sense that it is generally concealed. But that was far from the case in ancient Greece and Rome. At the gymnasium in ancient Greece, people exercised in the nude. In ancient Rome, men and women would bathe naked together.[7] In the Middle Ages, people bathed in front of others and during social gatherings.[8] Norms about nudity, bathing and concealing bodily functions have varied throughout history and in different cultures. Likewise, although the home has long been viewed as a private space, in the past it was private in a different way than it is now. Until the seventeenth century, many homes merely consisted of one large room where there was scant seclusion for 'private' activities such as sex and intimacy. A married couple would often sleep in the same bed as their children, and would share it with houseguests.[9] Like the body, the home is not inherently private – at least not in the same way we view it as private today.

Many theories of privacy focus on the nature of the information or matter involved. They seek to identify various types of information and matters that are private. But as I illustrated with the body and the home, no particular kind of information or matter is inherently private. Others contend that we should define privacy with the reasonable expectation of privacy test. This method defines privacy based on expectations that society considers reasonable. This is the prevailing method that American courts, as well as courts in many other countries and the European Court of Human Rights, use to identify privacy interests protected by the Fourth Amendment as well as other areas of law.[10]

But how are reasonable expectations of privacy to be determined? The US Supreme Court has never engaged in empirical evidence when applying the reasonable expectation of privacy test. It merely guesses at what society expects. One way of determining societal expectations is to take polls. But people's stated views about privacy often differ dramatically from their actions. A person might say she values privacy greatly, but then she'll trade away her personal data for tiny discounts or minor increases in convenience. For this reason, others contend that we should examine behavioural data rather than polls. There are several factors, however, that make people's behaviour unreliable as a measure for their views on privacy. In many circumstances, people relinquish personal information to businesses because they don't have much of a choice or because they lack knowledge about how the information will be used in the future.

7. Simon Goldhill, *Love, Sex, and Tragedy: How the Ancient World Shapes Our Lives* (Chicago, University of Chicago Press, 2004), p. 15, 19.

8. Witold Rybczynski, *Home: A Short History of an Idea* (New York: Penguin Books, 1986), 28, 30.

9. David H. Flaherty, *Privacy in Colonial New England* (Charlottesville: University Press of Virginia, 1972), 45.

10. H. Tomás Gómez-Arostegui, 'Defining Private Life Under the European Convention on Human Rights by Referring to Reasonable Expectations', *California Western International Law Journal*, vol. 35 (2005) no. 2, 153.

Even with a reliable way of measuring societal expectations of privacy, such expectations only inform us about existing privacy norms. Privacy law and policy depend on more than merely preserving current expectations. The history of communications privacy best illustrates this point. In colonial America, mail was often insecure. Letters, sealed only with wax, left many people concerned that they were far from secure. For example, Thomas Jefferson, Alexander Hamilton and George Washington all complained about the lack of confidentiality in their correspondence.[11] Despite the expectation that mail was not very private, the law evolved to provide strong protection of the privacy of letters. Benjamin Franklin, the colonial postmaster general before the Revolution, made postal workers take an oath not to open mail.[12] After the Revolution, the US Congress passed several statutes to protect the privacy of letters. In 1877, the US Supreme Court held that the Fourth Amendment protected sealed parcels despite the fact that people handed them to the government for delivery.[13] The extensive protection of the privacy of written correspondence stemmed from a public desire to keep them private, not from an expectation that they were already private.

A similar story can be told with electronic communications. Concerns over telegraph privacy were legion in its early days during the mid-nineteenth century. Laws in almost every state ensured that telegraph employees could not improperly disclose telegrams. State laws also prohibited the interception of telegraph communications. During the telephone's early days, calls were far from private. Until well into the twentieth century, many people had party lines – telephone lines that were shared among a number of households. There were rampant concerns about eavesdropping and wiretapping. Legislatures responded by passing laws to protect the privacy of phone communications. More than half the states had made wiretapping a crime by the early twentieth century.

The moral of the story is that communications *became* private because people wanted them to be private. Privacy is not just about what people *expect* but about what they *desire*. Privacy is something we construct through norms and the law. Thus, we call upon the law to protect privacy *because* we experience a lack of privacy and desire to rectify that situation, not because we already expect privacy.

What, then, should we focus on when seeking to understand privacy? I contend that the focal point for a theory of privacy should be on the problems we want the law to address. According to John Dewey, philosophical inquiry begins with problems in experience, not with abstract universal principles.

A theory of privacy should focus on the problems that create a desire

11. Daniel J. Solove, *The Digital Person: Technology and Privacy in the Information Age* (New York: New York University Press, 2004), 225.

12. Ibid.

13. Ex Parte Jackson, 96 U.S. 727, 733 (1877).

for privacy. Privacy problems arise when the activities of the government, businesses, organizations and other people disrupt the activities of others. Real problems exist, yet they are often ignored because they do not fit into a particular conception of privacy. Many problems are not even recognized because courts or policy-makers can't identify a 'privacy' interest involved. Instead of pondering the nature of privacy in the abstract, we should begin with concrete problems and then use theory as a way to better understand and resolve these problems. In my new book, *Understanding Privacy*, I develop a framework for recognizing privacy problems, and I identify and examine [16] such problems.

There are four basic groups of harmful activities: (1) information collection, (2) information processing, (3) information dissemination, and (4) invasion. Each of these groups consists of different related subgroups of harmful activities.

I have arranged these groups around a model that begins with the data subject – the individual whose life is most directly affected by the activities classified in the taxonomy. From that individual, various entities (other people, businesses and the government) collect information. The collection of this information itself can constitute a harmful activity, though not all information collection is harmful. Those that collect the data (the 'data holders') then process it – that is, they store, combine, manipulate, search, and use it. I label

these activities 'information processing'. The next step is 'information dissemination', in which the data holders transfer the information to others or release the information. The general progression from information collection to processing to dissemination is the data moving further away from the individual's control. The last grouping of activities is 'invasions', which involve impingements directly on the individual. Instead of the progression away from the individual, invasions progress towards the individual and do not necessarily involve information. The relationship between these different groupings is depicted in the figure.

The first group of activities that affect privacy is information collection. *Surveillance* is the watching, listening to, or recording of an individual's activities. *Interrogation* consists of various forms of questioning or probing for information.

A second group of activities involves the way information is stored, manipulated and used – what I refer to collectively as 'information processing'. *Aggregation* involves the combination of various pieces of data about a person. *Identification* is linking information to particular individuals. *Insecurity* involves carelessness in protecting stored information from leaks and improper access. *Secondary use* is the use of collected information for a purpose different from the use for which it was collected without the data subject's consent. *Exclusion* concerns the failure to allow the data subject to know about the data that others have about her and participate in its handling and use. These activities do not involve the gathering of data because it has already been collected. Instead, these activities involve the way data is maintained and used.

The third group of activities involves the dissemination of information. *Breach of confidentiality* is breaking a promise to keep a person's information confidential. *Disclosure* involves the revelation of truthful information about a person that affects the way others judge her reputation. *Exposure* involves revealing another's nudity, grief, or bodily functions. *Increased accessibility* is amplifying the accessibility of information. *Blackmail* is the threat to disclose personal information. *Appropriation* involves the use of the data subject's identity to serve another's aims and interests. *Distortion* consists of disseminating false or misleading information about individuals. Information-dissemination activities all involve the spreading or transfer of personal data or the threat to do so.

The fourth and final group of activities involves invasions into people's private affairs. Invasion, unlike the other groupings, need not involve personal information (although in numerous instances, it does). *Intrusion* concerns invasive acts that disturb one's tranquillity or solitude. *Decisional interference* involves incursion into the data subject's decisions regarding her private affairs.

Privacy is not one thing, but many distinct but related things. For too long, policymakers and others have viewed privacy too myopically and narrowly, failing to recognize many important privacy problems. Understanding privacy in a more pluralistic manner will hopefully improve the way privacy problems are recognized and addressed.

The Social Value of Privacy

Another problem with the way privacy is often conceptualized involves how its value is assessed. Traditional liberalism often views privacy as a right possessed by individuals. For example, legal theorist Thomas Emerson declares that privacy 'is based upon premises of individualism, that the society exists to promote the worth and dignity of the individual. . . . The right of privacy . . . is essentially the right not to participate in the collective life – the right to shut out the community.'[14] In the words of one court: 'Privacy is inherently personal. The right to privacy recognizes the sovereignty of the individual.'[15]

14. Thomas I. Emerson, *The System of Freedom of Expression* (New York: Vintage Books, 1970), 545, 549.

15. Smith v. City of Artesia, 772 P.2d 373, 376 (N.M. Ct. App. 1989).

Framing privacy exclusively in individualistic terms often results in privacy being under-valued in utilitarian balancing, which is the predominant way policymakers resolve conflicts between various interests. When individual interests are pitted against the common good, the latter often wins out. The interests often in tension with privacy – free speech, efficient consumer transactions, or security – are frequently understood as valuable for all of society. Privacy, in contrast, is seen as a zone of respite for the sake of the individual.

There is a way, however, to justify privacy from a utilitarian basis. Pragmatist philosopher John Dewey has articulated the most coherent theory of how protecting individual rights furthers the common good. For Dewey, there is no strict dichotomy between individual and society. The individual is shaped by society, and the good of both the individual and society are often interrelated rather than antagonistic: 'We cannot think of ourselves save as to some extent *social* beings. Hence we cannot separate the idea of ourselves and our own good from our idea of others and of their good.'[16] Dewey contended that the value of protecting individual rights emerges from their contribution to society. In other words, individual rights are not trumps, but are protections by society from its intrusiveness. Society makes space for the individual because of the social benefits this space provides. Therefore, Dewey argues, rights should be valued based on 'the contribution they make to the welfare of the community'.[17] Otherwise, in any kind of utilitarian calculus, individual rights would not be valuable enough to outweigh most social interests, and it would be impossible

16. John Dewey, *Ethics* (1908), in: Jo Ann Boydston (ed.), *John Dewey, the Middle Works, 1899-1924*, vol. 5 (Carbondale: Southern Illinois University Press, 1978), 268.

17. John Dewey, *Liberalism and Civil Liberties* (1936), in: Jo Ann Boydston (ed.), *John Dewey, the Later Works, 1925-1953*, vol. 11 (Carbondale: Southern Illinois University Press, 1987), 374.

to justify individual rights. As such, Dewey argued, we must insist upon a 'social basis and social justification' for civil liberties.[18]   18. Ibid. at 375.

I contend, like Dewey, that the value of protecting the individual is a social one. Society involves a great deal of friction, and we are constantly clashing with each other. Part of what makes a society a good place in which to live is the extent to which it allows people freedom from the intrusiveness of others. A society without privacy protection would be suffocating, and it might not be a place in which most would want to live. When protecting individual rights, we as a society decide to hold back in order to receive the benefits of creating the kinds of free zones for individuals to flourish.

As Spiros Simitis declares, 'privacy considerations no longer arise out of particular individual problems; rather, they express conflicts affecting everyone'.[19] Privacy, then, is not the trumpeting of the individual against society's interests but the protection of the individual based on society's own norms and practices. Privacy is not simply a way to extricate individuals from social control, as it is itself a form of social control that emerges from the norms and values of society.

19. Spiros Simitis, 'Reviewing Privacy in an Information Society', *University of Pennsylvania Law Review*, 707, 709 (1987), 135. In analysing the problems of federal legislative policy-making on privacy, Priscilla Regan demonstrates the need for understanding privacy in terms of its social benefits. See Priscilla M. Regan, *Legislating Privacy: Technology, Social Values, and Public Policy* (Chapel Hill, NC: The University of North Carolina Press, 1995), xiv ('An analysis of congressional policy making reveals that little attention was given to the possibility of a broader social importance of privacy.')

We protect individual privacy as a society because we recognize that a good society protects against excessive intrusion and nosiness into people's lives. Norms exist not to peak into our neighbour's windows or sneak into people's houses. Privacy is thus not an external restraint on society but is in fact an internal dimension of society.[20] Therefore, privacy has a social value. Even when it protects the individual, it does so for the sake of society. It thus should not be weighed as an individual right against the greater social good. Privacy issues involve balancing societal interests on both sides of the scale.

20. Robert C. Post, 'The Social Foundations of Privacy: Community and Self in the Common Law Tort', *California Law Review*, vol. 77 (1989), 957, 968 (arguing that privacy is society's attempt to promote norms of civility).

Because privacy involves protecting against a plurality of different harms or problems, the value of privacy is different depending upon which particular problem or harm is being protected. Not all privacy problems are equal; some are more harmful than others. Therefore, we cannot ascribe an abstract value to privacy. Its value will differ substantially depending upon the kind of problem or harm we are safeguarding against. Thus, to understand privacy, we must conceptualize it and its value more pluralistically. Privacy is a set of protections against a related set of problems. These problems are not all related in the same way, but they resemble each other. There is a social value in protecting against each problem, and that value differs depending upon the nature of each problem.

Clearing Away the Confusion

Understanding privacy as a pluralistic concept with social value will hopefully help add clarity and concreteness to a concept that has been shrouded in a fog of confusion for far too long. This conceptual confusion has caused policymakers to struggle to respond to the myriad emerging threats technology poses for privacy, from the rise of surveillance cameras to the extensive data trails created by the Internet and electronic commerce. With greater conceptual clarity in understanding the meaning and value of privacy, we can better tackle the difficult task of protecting privacy in the Information Age.

Matthijs Bouw

New Map of Tbilisi

Privatization and Privacy

Design firms FAST and One Architecture took the Georgian city of Tbilisi as the starting point for their research of the consequences of neoliberal developments.[1] The editors of *Open* asked Matthijs Bouw of One Architecture to make a presentation of their project 'New Map of Tbilisi' with photographic images by Gio Sumbadze and Lucas Zoutendijk. This shows how privatization has advanced the privacy of a few at the expense of the privacy of many.

1. See: www.newmapoftbilisi.org

After the 2003 Rose Revolution, Georgia plunged into a wild capitalism, exacerbated by the American neo-conservatives' use of the country for experiments in pure neoliberalism. Spatial planning became suspect, public assets were quickly privatized, and the city faced rampant land and property speculation.

This situation led FAST and One Architecture to team up with local artists to produce a 'New Map of Tbilisi'. The Map is an Internet platform (www.newmapoftbilisi.org) that exposes for the first time all spatial and infrastructural projects being imagined or built in Tbilisi. The collected plans are put together in one database, such that they can be shown on the map, analysed and acted upon. The Map shows that many of the city's public buildings and public areas have been sold off to developers, and how this process makes the city's current atomized development and the lack of strategic coherence worse.

In Tbilisi, the collective sphere of the Soviet Union made way for the individual, after its collapse. And after the Rose Revolution, what was public was replaced by the private. But in Tbilisi, individuality and privatization do not automatically mean more privacy. Our project shows how, with privatization, privacy is increased for the few, but reduced for the many.

Tbilisi used to be a pearl of the Soviet Union, a model city. Georgia was, after all, a favourite holiday destination of the Soviet elite. Its beautiful parks, public beaches and public buildings, however, fell into decay during the 1990s, a period marked by civil wars and a devastating earthquake.

The state of the city after this time is best illustrated by the Hotel Iveria, located on the central square of the city. This building used to express its collective function through its modernist design. In 2003, it was filled with refugees. Each of the original rooms was occupied differently. This was visible in a façade that looked like an MVRDV *avant la lettre*, a wild growth of individual modifications. While MVRDV's architecture signifies 'individuality' in Western Europe, it spells 'breakdown' in the Caucasus.

At the time of the Rose Revolution, like Hotel Iveria, much of Tbilisi's public buildings, its hotels, schools and hospitals, were occupied by refugees of the civil wars. Since then, the government has initiated a massive wave of privatization. In principle, according to neo-conservative theory, the government should limit itself to maintaining law and order, and defence. All else is sold off.

The government has since sold the Hotel Iveria and evacuated it. It has now been converted into the Radisson-Sas Hotel. The refugees (Internally Displaced People, or IDP's, in the parlance of the NGO-world) have been displaced again. The government sold many of the hospitals, offices and schools it owned, and evacuated them. The government has sold the parks and the beaches. Much of the former civic infrastructure is now in private hands, and in the process of being developed. The privatized assets form the basis of Tbilisi's real estate boom, the Map shows.

The shiny real estate developments are aimed at the new rich. They have security. They are gated. The formerly public beaches of both Tbilisi Sea and Lisi Lake will, as centres of new suburban and recreational developments, become accessible to the inhabitants of their newly privatized city only. Beneficiaries of privatization, they have the beach to themselves. In the centre, much of the former public buildings have become 'class A' apartment and office complexes.

And it is those areas that have been forcibly evacuated by the IDP's. Not only the IDP's from the civil wars, but also the IDP's of privatization. The rampant development of Tbilisi's city centre has meant that not only the refugees, but also many ordinary citizens have been displaced, and with them the unique social structures.

The IDP's can now be found in the new towns from the Chruchov-era, far from the centre. The collectivist blocks, and the public spaces between them have been occupied by refugees of wars and privatization. The conditions in the cramped quarters in which many people live or work often seem not much different from the conditions of Hotel Iveria just after the Civil War.

Apart from a concern for the city itself, FAST and One Architecture work on the New Map of Tbilisi because Tbilisi's experiment with neoliberalism provides clues about how the world might look like if capitalism goes unchecked. Tbilisi's experience makes clear that the 'tent cities'[2] that can be now found in the USA, as the result of foreclosures, are not an anomaly but as much a product of neoliberalism as privatopia is. And its shows that, in this condition, privacy is for the happy few.   2. See: thelede.blogs.nytimes.com/2009/03/11/tent-city-report/

www.newmapoftbilisi.org

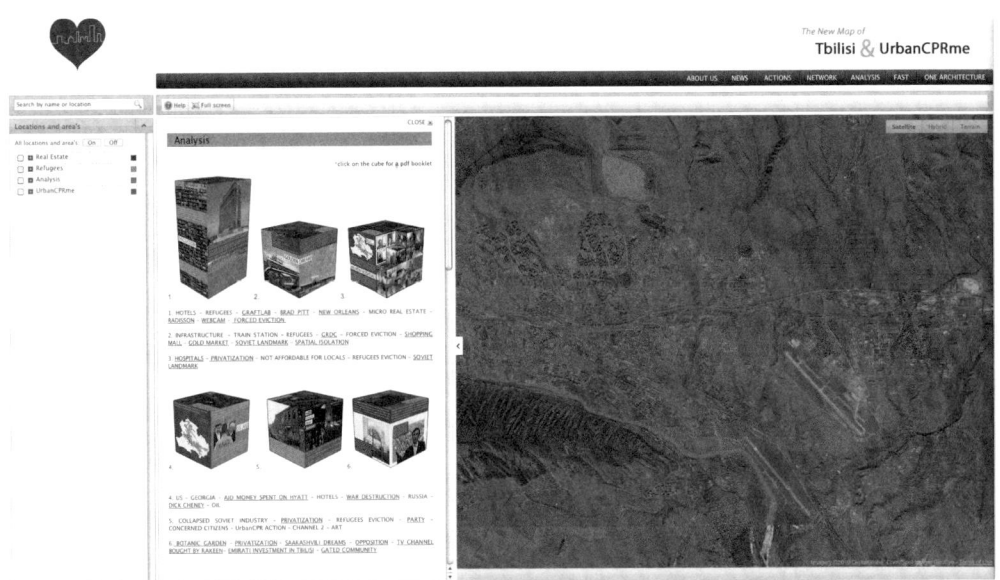

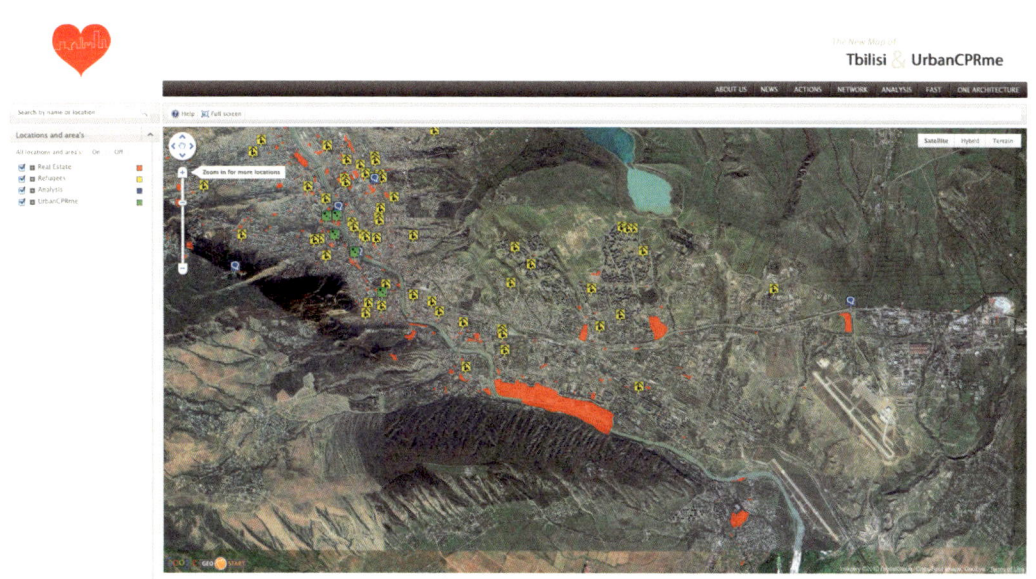

Gio Sumbadze, construction site Gldani district, 2009.

Gio Sumbadze, business center on former Komsomol alley, 2009.

Gio Sumbadze, cable car to the university campus, 2009.

Gio Sumbadze, construction site on Metekhi rock, 2009.

Gio Sumbadze, former publishing house, 2008.

Gio Sumbadze, former Soviet military hospital, 2008.

Gio Sumbadze, kiosk, 2009.

Gio Sumbadze, former Soviet military hospital, 2008.

Gio Sumbadze, IDP settlement, 2009.

New Map of Tbilisi

Gio Sumbadze, near Mziuri park, 2009.

Gio Sumbadze, settlement at the Vake-Saburtalo road, 2009.

Gio Sumbadze, Varketili metro station entrance, 2009.

Lucas Zoutendijk, public beach at Lisi Lake, 2009.

Lucas Zoutendijk, Tbilisi Heights, 2009.

Armin Medosch

Margins

of Freedom

Privacy and

the Politics

of Labour and

Information

Media artist, writer and curator Armin Medosch researches the development in the meaning of the term 'freedom' and the idea of privacy that goes with it. The solution to the current crisis concerning privacy stretches beyond finding a new balance between private and public. According to Medosch, the solutions should be sought in the realm of the digital commons, where freedom is not seen as something to achieve on one's own by accumulating possessions, but as something that is created by sharing knowledge.

'Privacy is the claim of individuals, groups or institutions to determine for themselves when, how and to what extent information about them is communicated to others.'[1] If we accept this definition, it is only too obvious how little control we have over information about ourselves.

1. Alan F. Westin, *Privacy and Freedom* (New York: Atheneum, 1967), 7, quoted in Beate Rössler, *Der Wert des Privaten* (Frankfurt am Main: Suhrkamp, 2001), 22.

The gathering of personalized information is not an involuntary by-product of technology but a key component of the way the 'information society' works. The rationale for information gathering stems partly from the 'need' of modern societies to have enough knowledge about themselves to keep functioning; but this involves further 'needs', such as to control labour, shape consumption and create a 'database state'. The foundational myths of the information age have inscribed themselves into the developmental path of information and communication technologies (ICT). While a desire for automated surveillance has long existed, it is now matched by an amplified capacity to actually carry it out.

A number of national and international campaign groups such as Foebud. e.V. in Germany, quintessenz.at in Austria, the EFF and ACLU in the USA, and the European umbrella organization EDRI are fighting the erosion of privacy. Some of them organize the annual 'Big Brother Awards' (BBA), where the worst anti-privacy measures are 'honoured'. In the UK, where the BBA was invented, the physical object awarded is a statue of a military boot stamping on a head. But the jackboot is not an image that

people living in liberal democracies associate with their reality. Warning against an outdated critique of totalitarianism doesn't mean that liberal democracies don't produce totalitarian techniques. This text tries to support effective strategies for counter-surveillance by developing a richer heuristic model, connecting the historic function of privacy in liberal democracies with the overall technopolitical dynamics fostering its rise then and its decline today.[2]

2. An effort to understand this 'overall dynamics' is made through the collaborative research project Technopolitics developed jointly by Brian Holmes, the author and others on http://www.thenextlayer. org.

Privacy in a Free Democracy

Privacy is an important category for the political-philosophical framework of liberalism[3] and has a constitutive function within the legal framework of liberal democracy by expressing the idea of the protection of individual freedom and autonomy from unjust intrusions or regulations of the state.[4] Out of the intimate as a nucleus of the private sphere, the public sphere was created by bourgeois citizen journalists, argues Habermas.[5] 'The public sphere of civil society . . . ultimately came to assert itself as the only legitimate source of [the] law.'[6] Habermas acknowledges that this

3. This conception of liberalism was formulated during the Great Englisch Revolution in the seventeenth century and philosophically in the work of John Locke. For a critique, cf. C.B. McPherson, *The Political Theory of Possessive Individualism: Hobbes to Locke* (Clarendon: OUP, 1962/2009).

4. Rössler, *Der Wert*, op. cit. (note 1), 27.

5. Jürgen Habermas, *The Structural Transformation of the Public Sphere: An Inquiry into a Category of Bourgeois Society* (Studies in Contemporary German Social Thought) (Cambridge, MA: MIT Press, 1989).

6. Ibid., 54.

political function of the public sphere could gain valency only once 'commodity exchange and social labour became largely emancipated from governmental directives'. The market, Habermas concludes, was 'the social precondition for a "developed" bourgeois public sphere'.[7]

E.P. Thompson's 7. Ibid., 73-74. account of the making of the English working class shows that the reading public was not restricted to the bourgeoisie.[8] Inspired by the French Revolution, 'English Jacobins' met in taverns and private houses, bookshops

8. E.P. Thompson, *The Making of the English Working Class* (Harmondsworth: Penguin, 1975).

and cafes to read revolutionary literature and demand political reforms. These 'plebeian radicals' placed high value on self-education, egalitarianism, rational criticism of religious and political institutions, a conscious republicanism and a strong internationalism.[9] The ruling class 9. Ibid., 199-201. reacted through the suspension of *habeas corpus* and a series of repressive laws such as the Seditious Meetings and Combination Acts. As a result, the 'plebeian radicals' were driven leftwards and underground,[10] so that they failed to create stronger 10. Ibid., 200. ties with those parts of the bourgeoisie who, under different conditions (no war with France, for example), might have sided with them. The early working class pre-configured many aspects of the working-class ideology after 1830, which held in high regard 'the rights of the press, of speech, of meeting and of personal liberty', writes Thompson, dismissful of the 'the notion to be found in some late "Marxist" interpretation' that these values have been inherited from 'bourgeois individualism'.[11]

The establish- 11. Ibid., 805. ment of the bourgeoisie as a privileged legal subject was based on legislation that enshrined into law the suppression of the English working class, argues Saskia Sassen.[12] Habermas's concept of the reasoning public is an idealization that needs to be called into question. Maybe the public sphere does not

12. Saskia Sassen, *Territory, Authority, Rights: From Medieval to Global Assemblages* (Princeton, NJ: Princeton University Press, 2006), 110 et passim, in particular footnote 66.

necessarily develop out of the intimacy of the private sphere but rather out of a political process of the shaping of class consciousness, whether between members of the bourgeoisie or a very diverse group of artisans, craftsmen and -women and labourers.

The particular conditions set by the early defeat of the English working class had a determining influence on the path of technological development out of antagonistic class relationships. A specific version of technological progress under capitalist conditions was set in motion, which sought direct control of workers at the site of production and the displacement of skilled human labour through machines. 'It is a result of the division of labour in manufacture that the worker is brought face to face with the intellectual potentialities of the material process of production as the property of another and as a power that rules over him,' wrote Karl Marx,[13] capturing a basic tendency that is still at work and has only intensified .

13. Karl Marx, *Capital* Vol I (city: publisher, 1976), 482.

Armand Mattelart[14] argues that an information-age-before-the-name started in France with Concordet's conception of statistics as a 'social physics' at the time of the French Revolution. Enlightenment philosophers made mathematical thinking the yardstick for 'judging the quality of citizens and the values of universalism'. From Concordet via the British tax system during the Napoleonic wars, the development of statistics leads in the course of the nineteenth century to an 'insurance society'[15] where the profitability of businesses and the success of governments depends on the ability to apply probabilistic 'technologies' for the prediction and management of the future.

14. Arman Mattelart, *The Information Society: An Introduction* (city: publisher, 2001), 5.

15. Ian Hacking, *The Taming of Chance* (Cambridge: Cambridge University Press, 1990).

The philosopher and historian of science Simon Schaffer sees a link between the 'growing system of social surveillance in Great Britain in the early 19th century and the emerging mechanisation of natural philosophies of mind'.[16] According to Schaffer the 'politics of intelligence' of the time located 'intelligence' in machinery and its conception, while at the same time the unity of manual and mental labour was broken. A key protagonist in this ideological battle was Charles Babbage, the designer of the 'difference engine' and the 'analytic engine'. Babbage was inspired by Gaspard de Prony's application of the principle of the division of labour to the task of converting old measurements

16. Simon Schaffer, BABBAGE'S INTELLIGENCE (2007), online: www.imaginaryfutures. net/2007/04/16/babbages-intelligence-by-simon-schaffer/, no pagination.

into the new uniform decimal system. Babbage's 'dream' was to implement such a division of labour in his calculating machines. The displacement of human mental labour by a machine was instantly connected with the analogy of artificial 'intelligence' by the circle around Babbage. This 'vision' was developed alongside an analogy between the internal organization of Babbage's mechanical calculators and the view of the mechanized factory as a Benthamite Panopticon. Babbage and other 'factory tourists' – middle-class intellectuals who travelled to the new factory districts in the north of England – gave accounts 'of the factory as a transparent and rational system designed to demolish traditional and customary networks of skill and artisan culture', reports Schaffer. Not only did the new factories make artisans unemployed, but their contribution to the development of new technologies was talked down to legitimize the existing class structure. The Babbage principle states: 'That the master manufacturer by dividing the work to be executed into different processes, each requiring different degrees of skill or of force, can purchase exactly that precise quantity of both which is necessary for each process.'[17]

17. Charles Babbage, *On the Economy of Machinery and Manufactures* (1832), quoted from Project Gutenberg: http://www.gutenberg.org/dirs/etext03/cnmmm11.txt.

This legacy contributes to the blueprint of the factory as well as the calculation engine, according to Schaffer. The early nineteenth-century 'politics of intelligence' can be understood as the forerunner of the project of artificial intelligence (AI) developed by the pioneers of the computer age, Turing,

Shannon, Von Neumann and Wiener.[18]

Harry Braverman's critique of Taylorism exposes the key principles that shaped the emergence of 'modern management'. Claiming Babbage as a direct forerunner of F.W. Taylor,[19] Braverman argues that the 'absolute necessity' to control each step of the labour process and its mode of execution makes necessary the creation of a monopoly of knowledge about the work process.[20] Management assumes 'the burden of gathering together all of the traditional knowledge which in the past has been possessed by the workmen and then of classifying, tabulating and reducing this knowledge to rules, laws, and formulae . . .'[21] This logic also requires that 'every activity in production have its several parallel activities in the management center'.[22] Parallel to the flow of things a flow of paper comes into existence, created by the new professional class of middle managers who are busy with the gathering of data, the planning, organization and supervision of production.[23] Their work is subjected to the same carefully occasioned fragmentation designed by top management to keep the strings of control tightly in their hands.[24] The 'flow of paper' created by the parallel work of planning has meanwhile been transformed into a flow of information:

18. Simon Schaffer, OK Computer (2007), online: www.imaginaryfutures. net/2007/04/16/ok-compu-ter-by-simon-schaffer/, no pagination.

19. Harry Braverman, *Labor and Monopoly Capital: The Degradation of Work in the Twentieth Century* (New York: Monthly Review Press, 1975), 89.

20. Ibid., 119-120.

21. F.W. Taylor, *The Principles of Scientific Management* (city: publisher, year), 111, quoted in Braverman, *Labor*, op. cit. (note 19), 112.

22. Braverman, *Labor*, op. cit. (note 19), 125.

23. Ibid., 126.

24. Ibid., 127.

the accumulated 'intelligence' of management encoded in software.

The introduction of mass production brought such increased levels of material flows, argues Beniger,[25] that it triggered a 'crisis of control' by the mid nineteenth century. The crisis gets resolved through the combination of a number of innovations such as the development of modern management, of modern accounting and the introduction of modern media such as the telegraph, telephone and typewriter. Together, they enable the creation of large-scale bureaucracy resulting in the particular form of organization embodied in the 'modern corporation'. There are strong co-dependencies in those techno-economic 'revolutions'. Railroads and the telegraph grow across the North American continent literally 'together'. The first companies to develop modern management techniques are themselves 'networks': railroad, telegraph and telephone networks.[26] The control revolution drives capitalism's hunger for 'information' and may provide a non or at least pre-military explanation for the need to invent the computer.

25. James R. Beniger, *The Control Revolution: Technological and Economic Origins of the Information Society* (Cambridge, MA: Harvard University Press, 1986).

26. Alfred D. Chandler, *The Visible Hand: The Managerial Revolution in American Business* (Cambridge, MA: Belknap Press, 1977).

From Fordism to Post-Fordism

When Fordism became the leading technological paradigm after the Second World War, it depended on certain macroeconomic stabilization factors which resulted in the requirement not only to control the production process but also the markets.[27] For the corporations, predicting and influencing future levels of consumption became a key part of their activity. In the early twentieth century a number of 'mass feedback' techniques were developed, such as market research, the Gallup poll, opinion surveys, indices of retail sales and Nielsen's radio rating.[28] New sociological schools started empirical research on 'the effects of media on receivers and the constant evolution of knowledge, behaviour, attitudes, emotions, opinions and actions'. This research was not purely academic but carried out in response to *practical objectives.*[29] 'The sponsors of those studies were concerned about the effects of government information campaigns, advertisement campaigns and army propaganda during wartime.'[30] The measurement of audiences with a view on regulating their behaviour as consumers and voters became the basis of what Brian Holmes calls Neilsenism, an interpretation of society as a cybernetic system with informational flows as control loops.[31] The notions of 'information', 'feedback' and 'systems' serve as an intermediate for a number of different processes which all depend on the gathering of 'information' about social properties of individuals and groups.

27. Michael J. Piore and Charles F. Sabel, *The Second Industrial Divide: Possibilities for Prosperity* (New York: Basic Books, 1984).

28. Beniger, *The Control*, op. cit. (note 25), 20.

29. Armand and Michèle Mattelart, *Theories of Communication: A Short Introduction* (London: Sage Publications, 1998), 28.

30. Ibid.

31. Brian Holmes, *Future Map or: How the Cyborgs Learned to Stop Worrying and Love Surveillance* (2007), online: brianholmes.word press.com/2007/09/09/future-map/

By the end of the 1960s Fordism enters a crisis resulting from the rigidities of the system, successful imitation by competitors and student and worker protest. From within the old techno-oeconomic paradigm a new paradigm based on microprocessors, telecommunications and information unfolds.[32] Concomitant with those shifts and transformations is the emergence of an advanced version of a more complex cybernetic system of control *and* seduction. More than ever the integration of feedback circuits into larger control systems relies on predictive algorithms, to paraphrase Brian Holmes. This upgraded paradigm of cybernetic control is no longer based on narrow functionalist and behaviourist ideas of 'manipulation'. Instead, it relies on more indirect, more internalized, more capillary forms of power and self-control. In the new postindustrial societies, the 'major professional preoccupation is pre-emptively shaping the consciousness of the consumer'.[33] The conditions of the networked society, the restructuring of management hierarchies, more decentralization, increased autonomy of workers in production and more individualism and freedom in society in general all point towards a greater margin of autonomy. The rise of financial markets, however, strengthens the capacity for the centralization of capital and power, making excessive use of informational tools for risk management. The atomized individuals are allowed to dance more freely as long as central power

32. Carlota Perez, *Technological Revolutions and Financial Capital: The Dynamics of Bubbles and Golden Ages* (Cheltenham, UK: E. Elgar Pub., 2002).

33. Holmes, *Future Map*, op. cit. (note 31).

functions are not affected or may even be better served by that increased margin of freedom.

In informational capitalism, the same technologies that appear to be fun and a vehicle for self-realization at the front-end have an entirely different dimension at the back-end. At the front-end, the aesthetics of the commodity[34] makes seductive promises about the use-value of goods. It is in the nature of informational capitalism to emphasize the front-end while hiding the back-end function. The relationship between front-end and back-end is in technical terms the one between server and client, both connected by the metaphor of the 'interface'. The interface can be a web-page for e-commerce or an e-government platform, or a cashier's desk in a bank or a retail store.

34. Wolfgang Fritz Haug, *Critique of Commodity Aesthetics: Appearance, Sexuality, and Advertising in Capitalist Society* (Minneapolis: University of Minnesota Press, 1986).

On the web, the 'empowerment' of the user on Web 2.0 platforms has been emphasized by many authors. Those platforms, however, are based on centralized server infrastructures, entirely under the control of the company hosting those social interactions. When it comes to harnessing the accumulation of knowledge, the server back-end is the privileged site. The techniques developed during the first decades of the twentieth century summarized under 'mass feedback' have become greatly enhanced through digitalization and the ready availability of user data in server log-files and on Internet exchanges. The automated analysis of data flows passing through networked information structures creates the new knowledge

of power. At the front-end this promises greater use-value: Amazon started it with proposing new books; Facebook automatically proposes new friends. At the server side ever more precise knowledge allows the targeting of individuals and their social networks based on data mining and 'profiling'. The user profiles, maps of individuals and their networked relationships, become tradable commodities themselves.

Shared Interests

With the increased pervasiveness of ICTs ever more areas in society have a dual existence as both virtual and real, the analogue space is connected to and interwoven with electronic space registering real-time information. The system of Just-In-Time production (JIT) is a key component of economic globalization which depends on tight control at the intersection of the virtual and the real. So-called 'logistics' or 'supply chain management' (SCM), stretches over continents and involves sophisticated technologies such as RFID tags to manage the flow of raw materials, manufactured parts and end products. Those many components are linked in such a way, that 'it can be argued that JIT production is responsible for the change in capitalist production from a push economy to a pull economy', writes Brian Ashton.[35] That means that when a customer takes a can of baked beans from a shelf at Tesco's the information is transmitted to all those along the supply chain

35. Brian Ashton, 'Logistics – Factory without walls', *Mute Magazine* (2006), online: www.metamute.org/en/Logistics-Factory-Without-Walls, (no pagination).

and the process to replace the item is put in motion. According to Ashton, workers in the logistics industries are 'bearing the brunt of the competitive pressures in those global supply chains', while their privacy is also compromised by new laws and regulations in the wake of 9/11. The International Ship and Port Facility Security Code enforced the building of visible and invisible security walls around ports. The police and security services have been given new rights to carry out checks on dock workers and to share information with foreign intelligence agencies.

The example of the logistics industry shows converging interests of the state and corporations to put workers under automated surveillance. The use of software with certain 'decision making support functions' at the front-end or the 'user interface' of businesses subjects both workers and consumers to the same surveillance logic. In jubilant stories in trade journals the benefits of new intrusive technologies called 'workforce management software . . . such as click-2staff' are being praised.[36] The software matches activity logs with customer statistics and produces automated recommendations for the allocation of staff according to 'overtime adherence' and 'salary adherence' policies.[37] One step further go products such as the Verint Witness Actionable Solutions, a package that promises to deliver 'actionable intelligence'[38] and to 'capture

36. Banktech.com, on 8 July 2002 Banks start to embrace workforce technology.

37. Cf. Bank of America Sucks, 10 January 2009, online: www.bankofameri-casucks.com/viewtopic.php?f=4&t=3295.

38. cominfosys.com/contact_center/section2a.cfm?article_level2_cat-egory_id=21&article_lev-el2a_id=273.

customer interactions in their entirety, selectively, on demand, or randomly'.

Verint is an industry leader in surveillance services working with 'law enforcement, national security, intelligence, and government agencies'. Their catalogue of services[39] is not so different from that of competitors such as Siemens Nokia, who promise to 'integrate data from many sources' such as 'data retention systems', 'Internet addresses merged with geographical information systems', 'traffic control points', 'credit card transactions' and 'DNA analysis database', to give just a few examples of a much longer list. The collation of data from such a diverse range of sources would be illegal in most European countries;[40] thus it highlights how the convergence of state and business interests in monitoring critical hubs of the network infrastructure deeply compromises privacy.

39. cominfosys.com/communications_interception/index.cfm.

40. Futurezone 03.04.2008 Das Siemens-Monster und die Legalitaet.

The European Data Retention Directive of 2006[41] mandates that all suppliers of telecommunications services keep the log-files of all communications of their users – not the actual content, but the 'who', 'when', 'where', type of meta-information – and that 'legal authorities' be granted automated access to it. Meta-information is actually much more useful for data mining than the 'noise' of content. The Austrian journalist Erich Möchel[42] is one among a

41. en.wikipedia.org/wiki/Directive_2006/24/EC.

42. Many of the examples in this section are based on Moechel's research, published on the website of quintessenz.at, cf. quintessenz.org/it_and_telco_surveillance_equipment.

number of investigative journalists who have uncovered the long trail of the secret backroom dealings which opened up a plethora of surveillance capacities at the business end of the net. For years, equipment manufacturers such as Siemens have been actively involved in working groups of the European Telecom Standards Institute (ETSI) who occupy themselves with defining the data handover-interface for Legal Interception. In other words, backdoors are being built systematically into equipment such as mobile phone switches and Internet routers, so that hardware-filtering devices can sift through the Internet traffic at speeds of 10 Gigabits per second and more. In EU funded research projects,[43] search engines are to be developed   43. www.indect-project.eu/. that combine all those data to automatically recognize 'abnormal behaviour' of 'mobile objects'.

As Saskia Sassen has noted, recent decades have seen a 'reconstruction of the divide' between the public and the private sphere 'partly through the policies of deregulation, privatization and marketization'.[44] Sassen argues that globalization strength-   44. Sassen, *Territory*, op. cit. (note 12), 184-185. ens the power of the executive branches of the state while it weakens the power of the legislative and therefore of democratic control. The privatization or deregulation of state tasks and responsibilities to private companies creates a move towards 'a privatized executive vis-à-vis the people and the other parts of government along with an erosion of citizens privacy'.[45] The other side of the coin is that the executive   45. Ibid., 184. grants itself ever more secrecy over its own decision-making. We can ask, with Saskia Sassen, what potentials exist to bring those tendencies to a tipping point where they can be reversed?

Digital Commons

This text has shown the usefulness of ICT for monopolizing knowledge and control in the hands of management and the executive branch of government. Some of the social forces shaping the path of development of technologies have been described. The systemic character of surveillance and dataveillance techniques at the workplace and in relation to consumers has been demonstrated. The automated detection of 'abnormal behaviour' binds together the data flows on the net with physical, spatial reality.

For all those reasons together, the problem is not simply to rebalance the private-public divide, but to find a more comprehensive answer to the current crisis of the information society. In the current transition, the digital commons opens a different path for economic and technological development. It should not be seen as a ready solution but more like a process that triggers other corresponding changes. Having originated from the Free Software movement in the 1980s, the digital commons has meanwhile found widespread support in the arts, culture, scientific publishing and research. As a new layer in societies that is growing from inside the most advanced sectors of cognitive capitalism, the digital commons offers new mechanisms for cooperation and

free association. For instance, if people work out of self-motivation rather than coercion, a big motivation for technically mediated control falls away. The digital commons reaches beyond the notion of software, information or informational cultural commodities.
It is a new way of doing things rather than a thing. It allows new alliances to be forged between digital commoners, knowledge workers, garage experimentalists, organic farmers, environmental activists and social movements. The digital commons is built on the recognition that freedom is not something that can best be attained individually through the possession of property, but collectively through the sharing of knowledge. But this proposal is necessarily incomplete, as the digital commons still faces many obstacles and challenges. Its further prospering is not a foregone conclusion, and its existence is owed to many patterns still associated with the old paradigm. However, the key point is that only a shift of such paradigmatic dimensions will get us off the hooks of the surveillance society.

Felix Stalder

Autonomy and Control in the Era of Post-Privacy

Researcher Felix Stalder analyses the loss of the key role of the concept of privacy. Privacy long secured the balance between the control of institutions and the autonomy of the citizen. Today, with institutions aiming more and more to provide customized services and the autonomy of both citizens and institutions changing, this role is disappearing, making the danger of an increase in control and power a realistic one. To turn the tide, Stalder argues for a greater transparency of the back-end protocols, algorithms and procedures of the new, flexible bureaucracies.

One way to characterize Western modernity, the period we are just leaving, is by its particular structure of control and autonomy. It emerged as the result of two historic developments – one leading to large, hierarchic bureaucracies as the dominant form of organization, the other to the (bourgeois, male) citizen as the main political subject. Privacy played a key role in maintaining a balance between the two. Today, this arrangement is unravelling. In the process, privacy loses (some of) its social functions. Post-privacy, then, points to a transformation in how people create autonomy and how control permeates their lives.

Bureaucracies and Citizens, 1700-1950

The first of these developments was the expansion of large-scale institutions, first state bureaucracies, then, since the late nineteenth century, commercial corporations.[1] Their attempts to organize social processes on a previously unimaginable scale – in

1. Alfred D. Chandler, Jr., *The Visible Hand: The Managerial Revolution in American Business* (Cambridge, MA/London: Harvard University Press, 1977).

terms of space, time and complexity – required vast amounts of information about the world, most importantly about the subjects in their domain. In 1686, the Marquis de Vauban proposed to Louis XIV a yearly census of the entire population, so that the king would be 'able, in his own office, to review in an hour's time the present and past condition of a great realm of which he is the head, and be able himself to know with certitude in what consists his grandeur, his wealth, and his strengths.'[2] At the time, such an endeavour could not be conducted for practical reasons, but the

2. Quoted in: James C. Scott, *Seeing Like a State: How Certain Schemes to Improve the Human Condition Have Failed* (Yale: Yale University Press, 1998), 11.

vision spawned an entire range of new theoretical approaches to render the world available in such a way. In 1749, the German political scientist Gottfried Achenwall (1719-1772) brought them together under the term 'statistics', defined as the 'science dealing with data about the condition of a state or community'. Yet, handling such data became ever more difficult as the drive to collect intensified. In the late nineteenth century, the US census, held once a decade, reached a critical juncture when the processing of the data amassed could not be finished before the next census was to be held. The historian James Beniger put this 'control crisis' at the beginning of the computer revolution and the information age enabled by it.[3] Without the systematic gathering of standardized information and its processing into actionable knowledge, none of the

3. James R. Beniger, *The Control Revolution: Technological and Economic Origins of the Information Society* (Cambridge, MA: Harvard University Press, 1986).

functions of the modern state, or the modern economy, could have developed, beginning with centralized taxation, standing armies, social welfare provisions, or international trade and production of complex goods and services. Thus, modernity, and particularly high modernity, was characterized by an expansion of control by large bureaucracies based on massive amounts of information, conceptualizing people as standardized datapoints to be manipulated for their own, or someone else's, good. But as long as life was lived in a largely analogue environment, the comprehensive gathering of data remained such an extremely labour-intensive affair that only massive bureaucracies were capable of conducting it, and even highly developed states could do it only once every ten years. Under such conditions of limited information processing capacity (as we can see now), the drive to scale up these bureaucracies created strategies to radically reduce complexity, rendering them rigid and impersonal.

Yet, during the same period of expanding centralized control, new spaces of autonomy were created. People, or, more precisely, educated townsmen, forged a new type of subjectivity. They began to think of themselves less as members of larger collectives (the guild, the church) and more as persons individually endowed with capacities, self-responsibility and, thus, a certain freedom from these collective entities. Central to this new sense of individuality was the secular notion of an inner life.[4]

It was characterized by the innate capacity to reflect and reason. This is, perhaps, *the* central notion of the enlightenment which celebrated the ability 'to use one's understanding without guidance from another', to

4. Charles Taylor, *Sources of the Self: The Making of the Modern Identity* (Cambridge, MA: Harvard University Press, 1989).

use Immanuel Kant's famous definition (1784). While these capacities were located in the inner world of the individual, the enlightenment thought of them as universal. In principle, every man (though not necessarily women) should reach the same reasoned conclusion, if presented with the same evidence. Based on this universality of reason, the subject could justifiably contradict authority and tradition.

The notion of privacy protected this inner world (and by extension, the home and the family life) from interference by authorities and thus protected the ability of the person to come to reasoned opinions about the world. In the liberal conception, this protected inner world provided the foundation of the ability of each man to form his own opinions to be exchanged in the public sphere in a rational deliberation of public affairs.[5]

This capacity for reasoning, in turn, provided the legitimacy for the inclusion of these reasoned men (and later women), elevated to the status of citizens, in governing the state. Indeed, this claim to power was increasingly regarded as the only legitimate one, superseding tradition as the main source of authority. Much of the concerns about the loss of privacy today stems from a commitment to this tradition of liberal democracy.[6]

5. Jürgen Habermas, *The Structural Transformation of the Public Sphere: An Inquiry into a Category of Bourgeois Society*, translated by Thomas Burger with the assistance of Frederick Lawrence (Cambridge, MA: MIT Press, 1989 [1962]).

6. See, for example, Wolfgang Sofsky, *Privacy: A Manifesto*, translated by Steven Rendall (Princeton and Oxford: Princeton University Press, 2008),

Starting in the late nineteenth century, however, the conception of the inner world changed radically. With the emergence of consumer capitalism, personal identity became a project and a problem with an urgency previously unknown. Inner life was no longer viewed as comprised of a relatively narrow set of coherent universals, but as an infinite expanse of conflicting drives and influences, forming a dynamic pattern unique to each person. Sigmund Freud, as the historian of psychoanalysis Eli Zaretsky argues, became the leading interpreter of the psychological tensions triggered by the consumer society.[7] The inner world came now to be seen as the ground on which individual identity (rather than universal reason) was anchored. Privacy protected the complex, and potentially dangerous exploration conducted by the individual as he or she tried to come to terms with the pressures and desires at the core of individuality. If we follow Zaretsky's approach of charting the transformation of subjectivities (and of psychoanalysis as the conceptual framework to articulate one type of it) alongside the transformations of capitalism, the type of subjectivity described by Freud started to lose its dominance in the 1960s.

New social movements began to react to the pressures and opportunities created by yet another transformation, towards what was then called the *post-industrial society* and is now called, more accurately, the *network society*. Rather than focusing on introspection, the new social movements promoted a new type of subjectivity emphasizing expressiveness, communication and connection. At the same time, feminists began to develop a sustained critique of privacy, understanding family relations not as the counteracting force to capitalism, but rather as its continuation. Thus, privacy would not shield from domination, but transfer it from the field of economics to that of gender relations.[8] However, despite the emergence of these freedom-oriented social movements, hierarchical bureaucracies remained the dominant form of social organization, and despite the feminist critique of privacy, it could still function as an important concept to shield people against the grip of these institutions. In Germany, for example, popular resistance against the national census (*Volkszählung*) arose in the mid 1980s, mainly on grounds of privacy protection against the preying eyes of the state.

Networked Individualism and Personalized Institutions

Fast forward 30 years. Many countries, including Germany, no longer conduct national censuses because the data has already been collected

or, if you read German, Beate Rössler, *Der Wert des Privaten* (Frankfurt am Main: Suhrkamp, 2001).

7. Eli Zaretsky, *Secrets of the Soul: A Social and Cultural History of Psychoanalysis* (New York: Vintage, 2005).

8. Catherine MacKinnon, *Toward a Feminist Theory of the State* (Cambridge, MA: Harvard University Press, 1989).

and can be aggregated flexibly from the various databases at the heart of government. An ever growing number of people is willing to actively publish vast amounts of information about themselves online for everyone to see and is happily using services that collect very fine-grained data about very personal affairs. While people still claim to be concerned about privacy when asked in surveys, their practices seem to indicate that such concerns have largely vanished in daily life. What happened? Here, I want to focus on two pieces of this puzzle. The first concerns the transformation of subjectivity on a mass scale. The second the changing relationships between individuals and institutions concerning the delivery of person- alized, rather than standardized services.[9]

9. I have addressed the role of the preven- tive security regimes elsewhere. Felix Stalder, 'Bourgeois Anarchism and Authoritarian Democ- racies', *First Monday*, vol. 13 (2008) no. 7 (July).

First, subjectivity. The values of the social movements of the 1960s, severed from their political roots, have spread throughout society. They are now dominant. Flexibility, creativity and expressiveness are regarded today as generally desirable personal traits, necessary for social success, and, increasingly, seen as corresponding to the 'true nature' of human beings. As traditional institutions are losing their ability to organize people's lives (think of the decline of life-long employment, for example), people are left to find their own orientation, for better or worse. While this has often been seen as primarily a negative process of atomization,[10] we can now also see new forms of sociability emerge on a mass scale. These are based on the new infrastructures of communication and (relatively) cheap transportation to which vast amounts of people have gained access. But the sociability in this new environment is starkly different from earlier forms, based largely on physical co-presence. In order to create sociability in the *space of flows* people first have to make themselves visible, that is, they have to create their representation through expres- sive acts of communication. In order to connect within such a network, a person has to be, at the same time, suitably different, that is creative in some recognizable fashion, and abide by the social conventions that hold a particular network together. There are both negative and positive drivers to making oneself visible in such a way: there is the threat of being invis- ible, ignored and bypassed, on the one hand, and the promise of creating a social network really expressing one's own individuality, on the other. This creates a particular type of subjectivity that sociologists have come to call *networked individualism*. 'Individuals,' Manuel Castells notes, 'do not withdraw into the isolation of virtual reality. On the contrary, they expand their sociability by

10. The classic here is: Robert Putnam, *Bowling Alone: The Collapse and Revival of American Community* (New York: Touchstone Books/ Simon & Schuster, 2000). A recent addition to this perspective: Jacqueline Olds and Richard S. Schwartz, *The Lonely American: Drifting Apart in the Twenty-First Century* (New York: Beacon Press, 2009).

using the wealth of communication networks at their disposal, but they do so selectively, constructing their cultural worlds in terms of their preferences and projects, and modifying it according to their personal interests and values.'[11] Since these networks of sociability are horizontal forms of organization, based on self-selected, voluntary associations, they require some degree of trust among the people involved. While trust deepens over the course of interaction, as it always does, there needs to be a minimum of trust in order to start interacting in the first place. What could be a chicken-and-egg problem is in practice solved by the availability of the track record of interests and projects that each person creates by publishing – as an individual and voluntarily – information about him/herself, what he or she is interest in, passionate about, and investing time in. In other words, being expressive – about anything – is the precondition of creating sociability over communication networks, which, in turn, come to define people and their ability to create or participate in projects that reflect their personality.[12] This need to express one's desires and passions in order to enter into a sociability that creates one's identity slowly but surely erodes the distinction between the inner and outer world, so central to the modern

11. Manuel Castells, *Communication Power* (Oxford: Oxford University Press, 2009), 121.

12. Christophe Aguiton and Dominique Cardon, 'The Strength of Weak Cooperation: An Attempt to Understand the Meaning of Web 2.0', *Communications & Strategies*, no. 65 (2007).

subjectivity, forged in the Gutenberg Galaxy. Subjectivity is being based on interaction, rather than introspection. Privacy in the networked context entails less the possibility to retreat to the core of one's personality, to the true self, but more the danger of disconnection from a world in which sociability is tenuous and needs to be actively maintained all of the time. Otherwise, the network simply reconfigures itself, depriving one of the ability to develop one's personality and life.

Second, large institutions. One of the progressive promises of the modern liberal state, and modern bureaucratic institutions in general, was to do away with privilege and treat everyone equally, based on the premise that no one is above (or below) the law and that all decisions are taken in accordance to the law (or, more generally, written procedure). Rigidity and impersonality have long been defined as core features of bureaucracies. Max Weber, at the beginning of the twentieth century when bureaucracies grew to an unprecedented scale, famously feared that their superior rationality would force society into an *iron cage*. Today, such impersonality is seen neither as a liberation from the injustices of privilege nor as rational, but as the dead hand of bureaucracy. Because, neoliberal ideology holds, we are not equal, but each unique. This creates both a push and a pull profoundly transforming the relationships between institutions and individuals. Even very large institutions are faced with demands to treat everyone individually. This is best visible in new institutions that have had to contend with these demands since their inception. The corporations that make up Web 2.0 are all about personalization, recommendations and individualized results. For that, they demand vast amounts of personal data, either directly provided by the user (by filling out registration forms, uploading personal contact lists and calendars, designating favourites and exchange partners) or indirectly collected (through log-analysis, processing of user histories, etcetera). Google, of course, is the most ambitious in this area, but in principle, it's not different from other Internet companies.[13]

But this is not an isolated development in one sector, but symptomatic for the uneven transformation of the economy as a whole. On the level of manufacturing, this is expressed in the shift from the Fordist model of standardized mass production to a networked model of highly flexible production for precisely defined niches, all the way down to the size of one. On the level of services, this is expressed in the shift towards the delivery of personalized services. Virtually all consumer-oriented industries and services are today employing customer-relationship management (CRM) vastly increasing the amounts of personal data collected across the board, allowing the delivery of highly targeted products and services. Of course, there is also a very strong pull by the corporations themselves to learn as much as possible about their customers/users, in order to fine-tune each relationship to maximize profit. There seems to be an implicit deal, accepted by the vast majority of consumers/users: in exchange for personal data, one receives personal service, assuming that personalized is better than standardized. In order to succeed in such an environment, bureaucracies, even large-scale ones, strive to become less hierarchical, more flexible and highly personal, entering into intimate relationships with the people they deal with.

Autonomy and Control

The old balance between autonomy and control, represented by the figures of the citizen and the large bureaucracy, sustained by privacy, is in the process of disappearing. Autonomy is increasingly created within (semi)public networks, held together by mass self-communication and more or less frequent physical encounters.[14] New projects to increase autonomy – that is the ability for people to lead their own lives according to their own plans – are being created on all scales and with the greatest variety of definitions of

13. For an analysis of Google's comprehensive data-gathering strategy, see Felix Stalder and Christine Mayer, 'The Second Index: Search Engines, Personalization and Surveillance', in: Konrad Becker and Felix Stalder (eds.), *Deep Search: The Politics of Search beyond Google* (Innsbruck/New Jersey: Studienverlag/Transaction Publishers, 2009), 98-116.

14. For the relationship between communication and travel, see Jonas Larsen, John Urry and Kay Axhausen, *Mobilities, Networks, Geographies* (Aldershot: Ashgate, 2006).

what autonomy actually looks like. What is characteristic to all of them is that the condition for autonomy is no longer understood as being rooted in the inner world, withdrawn from the social world, but in networked projects deeply engaged in the social world. Such projects range from the global justice campaigns, to the resurgence of local identities, from loosely coordinated political pressure campaigns to support groups that help people cope with personal traumas. They can be left-wing or right-wing, destructive or nurturing. Engagement in such projects is voluntary and they are held together by common protocols of communication and based on trust among their participants. Trust, in turn, is enabled by the horizontal availability of personal information about each other. In some ways, the dynamics of traditional offline communities – where everyone knows everyone – are being transported, transformed and scaled-up to new communities based on online communication. Of course, what 'knowing a person' means is rather different, and often distributed communities are too large to even superficially 'know' or count as a 'friend' everyone involved. Yet, if need be, everyone can be looked up and become suitably known very quickly, because everyone, voluntarily or involuntarily, leaves personal traces than can be accessed in real time or after the fact with great ease. While this, in itself, is not an entirely unproblematic condition – what about the freedom to have certain acts fade from memory?[15] – it provides the basis for the rise of new voluntary associations. This can help to increase real autonomy of people, because it is focused on creating inter-personal worlds in which autonomy can be lived on a daily basis, even if its extends only to some fraction of one's life.

15. Viktor Mayer-Schoenberger, *Delete: The Virtue of Forgetting in the Digital Age* (Princeton: Princeton University Press, 2009).

More problematic is the shift towards personalized institutions. With the rising complexity of the services delivered, personalization does have its benefits and the dead hand of bureaucratic formalism often can be, indeed, rather deadly. Yet, personalization also increases the power and control that such institutions can exercise, rather than the opposite. All the knowledge that goes into framing the character of the personalization resides at the end of the corporation that gets an ever increasing range of tools to fine-tune each relationship to optimize the pursuit of its own interests (usually profit maximization). As long as the actions of the user/customer are aligned with those of the corporation, they are supported and amplified through the granting of privileges, such as discounts, extra features and opportunities, faster delivery, and so on. However, as soon as the actions are no longer aligned (because they are hostile or not profitable), personalization turns into discrimination, based on whatever mechanisms are programmed into the underlying algorithms.[16] For the user, confronted with subtle, entirely opaque and unaccountable decision-making mechanisms, it

16. David Lyon (ed.), *Surveillance as Social Sorting: Privacy, Risk and Automated Discrimination* (London/New York: Routledge, 2003).

is nearly impossible to tell if one is being privileged or discriminated. There is no more standard against which this can be measured.

Thus, the possibilities to create meaningful autonomy are being expanded through voluntary, horizontal associations that directly express their members' interests and desires. At the same time and through the same infrastructure, the return of privileges and discrimination expands the ability of institutions to subtly or overtly shape other people's lives according to their agendas. Thus, we can observe a structural transformation of the conditions for autonomy as well as the practices of control. Privacy no longer serves to mediate between them. What should replace it are two things. New strategies for connective opacity extending both horizontally – modulating what those outside a particular network can see of what is going on inside – and vertically – modulating what the providers of the infrastructure can see of the sociability they enable. In a way, this can be seen as privacy 2.0, but it takes as its unit not the individual, but an entire social network. But that is not enough. We also need mandatory transparency of the protocols, algorithms and procedures that personalize the behaviour of these newly flexible bureaucracies, so that the conditions of discrimination can be contested.

column

JORIS VAN HOBOKEN

THE IMPORTANCE OF PRIVACY
CONFUSION ABOUT THE CIVIL RIGHT OF THE TWENTY-FIRST CENTURY

'Privacy is dead. Get over it.'[1]

One of the most interesting aspects of privacy is that it remains a burning issue around the world, even though it has already been declared dead a number of times. The debate on the penchant of governments and businesses to collect personal information, along with the introduction of more and more new technologies, attracts broad public interest in the Netherlands as well. Unfortunately, it is still not clear what the debate actually revolves around. The fact of the matter is, a great deal of confusion exists about what privacy really means. This confusion sometimes makes us forget what privacy has to offer as an ideal – also, and perhaps especially, for people in the twenty-first century.

In academic circles, theorists agree that it is a hopeless task to define privacy unequivocally. Privacy, so goes the conclusion, can better be seen as a hodgepodge of related values in differ-

1. For example, see: Pete Cashmore, 'Privacy is dead, and social media hold smoking gun.' CNN.com, 28 October 2009, edition. cnn.com/2009/ OPINION/10/28/cashmore.online.privacy/index.html.

ent contexts.[2] For instance, privacy safeguards physical integrity, control over personal information, the inviolability of the home and the confidentiality of communications. In turn, these principles can be based on the fundamental principle of the autonomy of the individual at the personal, intellectual and social levels.

2. For this conclusion and a good summary of the discussion, see: Daniel J. Solove, *Understanding Privacy* (Cambridge, MA: Harvard University Press, 2008).

Of course, the way in which the general public understands privacy is also important for the protection of privacy. The current public debate revolves in particular around the concept of 'informational' privacy. The focus is on everyone's right to have control over information referring to themselves. What is striking here is that privacy is usually understood to mean the extent to which information is divulged to others, instead of the amount of control over the sharing and use of this information. Privacy in the pubic debate stands for personal and confidential. Valuing privacy goes together with taking active measures to keep information about yourself hidden.

When privacy is understood in this light, it's not surprising that it has been declared dead many times. The amount of information divulged to others has increased immensely as a consequence of technology, new media and changing social notions. Information technology makes data recordable, controllable and usable at an unprecedented scale. The low threshold of the new media makes everybody in the Netherlands a potential celebrity. And fortunately, it is no longer a matter of course for people to keep secret about certain aspects of their personal identity, such as a non-heterosexual nature, on the grounds of a social taboo.

Understanding privacy as the extent to which information about yourself is revealed to others not only leads to tossing privacy into the wastebasket when it comes to concepts that are past their shelf life, it also leads to a subjectifying of the importance ascribed to privacy. In a constant stream of research and reports in the media, the importance of privacy is analysed in terms of how much people actually still value 'their' privacy. The Internet and social networks are pre-eminently suited for answering this question in negative terms. After all, so goes the reasoning, the mass use of social networks like Facebook and its Dutch equivalent, Hyves, is in itself already sufficient evidence to conclude that the importance of privacy has declined. Indeed, the 'Big Brother Award' that Bits of Freedom bestowed upon Dutch citizens in 2007 was interpreted by many people as a hint to use social networks.[3] A call to assess privacy at its

true value as a basic freedom and social principle was thus reduced to a call for confidentiality.

3. See: 'Winner Dutch Big Brother Awards 2007: "You"', 26 September 2009, Bits of Freedom, www.bigbrother awards.nl/ index_uk.html.

But the importance of privacy cannot be answered with the question of how people make use of 'their' right to privacy. Privacy gives people the right to choose what personal information they divulge and what they do not. After this data has been handed over to others, privacy also guarantees that it is used carefully and that people have a say in its use. And privacy as a civil right in principle offers people the freedom to make these choices without the prevailing social view on the correct use of this freedom being the deciding factor. Privacy is even a fundamental prerequisite for social diversity. It offers people the freedom to be, think and act differently without having to be afraid that this will have negative consequences on their social or financial position. The luxury of the feeling of having 'nothing to hide' is nothing more than that, a luxury. This relative luxury does not alter the fact that others might be vulnerable who are worth protecting.

It is quite possible that an inadequate protection of privacy has led to people being laconic about that right. The Dutch research project 'Nothing to hide and still afraid' indicates a general feeling of resignation among the Dutch population about the processing of their per-

sonal informa-
tion.[4] Considering
the value that
personal informa-
tion has acquired
for the business
world and the gov-
ernment in recent
decades, it is
hard to see this
as anything other than an indication
that the present right to 'informational' privacy apparently has little to offer Dutch citizens.

Yet privacy as a civil right and
social ideal is more relevant than
ever. The challenge is to make the
protection of privacy effective.
Divulging and sharing information
is a condition for social participation in the highly individualized
information society of the twenty-
first century. Information technology
enables the government and businesses to profile citizens and consumers, and to make strategic decisions at the individualized level.
Privacy can continue to guarantee
our control over how these processes
are set up, for example by further
sharpening the right to have access
to our personal data and the right
to information about how this data
is used. This can ensure that people remain central in a society tied
together by databases.

4. See: Regional
Plan, 'Niets te ver-
bergen en toch bang.
Nederlandse burg-
ers over het gebruik
van hun gegevens in
de glazen samen-
leving'. Final
report, January
2009, Amsterdam,
www.cbpweb.nl/down-
loads_rapporten/
rap_2009_niets_te_
verbergen_en_toch_
bang.pdf.

Bucharest Biennale 4

Bucharest International Biennial for Contemporary Art

May 21– July 25 2010

Bienala Internaţională de Artă Contemporană Bucureşti

21 Mai– 25 Iulie 2010

Handlung. On Producing Possibilities

Curated by Felix Vogel

Co-directed by Răzvan Ion & Eugen Rădescu

Generated by Pavilion - journal for politics and culture

www.bucharestbiennale.org I www.pavilionmagazine.org

Oliver Leistert

On Data Retention, Post-Fordism and Privacy Movements in Germany

The introduction of the data retention policy in the EU, resulting in digital doubles, has led to the emergence of grassroots protests centred on privacy and surveillance issues, especially in Germany. One of these, AK Vorrat, is a network platform that makes intensive use of the Internet and is rooted in the liberal democratic tradition. In the following text, media researcher Oliver Leistert places data retention in a post-Fordist framework and highlights some of the shortcomings of the protest movement.

The Directive

The 2006/24/EC directive was published on 21 February 2006, officially as a means to harmonize the market of data retention. This prompted Ireland to make a court appeal against the directive, with the argument that it is aimed at crime prevention, not market harmonization. Ireland seems to have a point. The directive aims to retain the connection data of all electronic tele-communication within the European Union for six to 24 months.[1] The connection data to be retained is the information necessary to:

1. A deeper analysis is undertaken in: Oliver Leistert, 'Data Retention in the European Union: When a Call Returns', *International Journal of Communication* 2 (2008), 925-935.

– trace and identify the source of a communication;
– identify the destination of a communication;
– identify the date, time and duration of a communication;
– identify the type of communication;
– identify users' communication equipment or what purports to be their equipment;
– and to identify the location of mobile communication equipment.

The responsibility of retaining this data is allocated to the telecom-munication companies. Some of these companies in Germany have criticized the directive, pointing to data protection concerns, but also to the additional costs for them and their customers, arguing that data retention is a state interest and should be financed by the state.

Only data concerning the content of telecommunications is not allowed to be retained. But what is content and what is not? This is a pretty arbitrary distinction in modern communication technology. Calling the emergency number is not about ordering pizza. Email headers are an integral part of emails. SMS is an even denser stream of data. The distinction of what is content and what is not in telecom-munications is a political project in itself. The idea of classification serves governing purposes. This aspect has been neglected in most considerations so far. Traditional surveillance by law enforcement agencies needs the permission of a judge, proof that the parties under surveillance are, for instance, criminal suspects, thus assuming that the content of their communications has something to do with their illegal activities. A discrimination between the content and metadata of this communication would not have made any sense. On a concep-tual level, therefore, the data retention scheme is an innovation, as it is not after specific suspects.

The data retention directive introduces this discrimination of data as a standard for all future telecommunications. Of course, this can be read as a balancing act between privacy and law enforcement interests. It is also a compromise to what is technically viable. Retaining all voice communication might not be viable yet, whereas retaining complete SMS communication is. In addition, the retained data is mostly data that is technically necessary for the communication services to function. This implies that most of this functional data is generated automatically at some point before, during or after the communication act in the technological infrastructure and only needs to be copied to be retained. Relying on the functional necessity of this automatically generated data, the directive is not based on principles but on technique, it is a *parasite* of technology. At the same time it introduces this distinction of data into the legal sphere, which has so far only played a role in billing and direct marketing, and even there with much less detailed data.

Making the doubling of information the institutional default plays into the hands of the industry of content production and that of copyright infringement prosecutors, who are lobbying intensively to get access to this data. Internet service providers and telecommunications companies also articulated an interest in this data (for marketing this is a goldmine). So, in a sense it's true, market harmonization does play a role here.

Mapping of Social Relations

What will be produced by this data retention scheme is a one-to-one mapping of all social relations passing through telecommunication technology. At least this is the wet dream of top-down bureaucrats. Starting from difficulties in standardization and technology hiccups, the problems the messy reality provides are numerous. And then, the means to circumvent data retention are at hand too, for those who care. Disregarding these difficulties, the idea of the data retention directive is to have access to the entire technologically mediated social fabric of the EU. The mapping of social networks via telecommunications is already a paradigm to make profit. Websites such as Facebook made this their business model, being fed with all this information by their content providers/users. In that sense, the EU and its stakeholders seem to only want their fair market share.

The powers of data retention are easy to sketch: a person receives a notice from the police about a person she communicated with half a year ago who now, according to them, is involved in crime. Most likely she will not remember the call or its contents. Maybe she cannot even remember this person. But it is all there on record and thus valid. Her virtual life strikes back, powerful and disintegrated from her physical existence. She has a *Doppelgänger* she can not control or get full knowledge about.

It echoes the physical presence of a person (well, at least that of her communication devices), since location data is also retained for all successful or non-successful acts of telecommunication. This adds a grid to the matrix of the doubled existence: the x and y axis. And z, the time-line, is also provided. GPS data, sent by default by more and more mobile phones to the nearest cell, narrows this down to a couple of metres.

Privacy

Google's CEO Eric Schmidt has openly stated that privacy has become impossible in all electronic communication and that the only way to regain privacy is to stay off the grid. This expression was critized as his personal, cynical view. But he has a point. The concept of privacy itself is changing with modern technology. Privacy is not all of a sudden under threat. It is a concept that is neither a-historical, nor universal. Rooted in Western liberalism, it never was global. It is a cornerstone of a specific ideology and therefore always in flux. It has an important function in the ideology of liberal democracy, occupying a similar space as the concept of free speech. It is an integral part of the idea of the liberal democratic state, a distinctive marker to differ-entiate it from totalitarianism. Privacy in its broadest sense is a state-sanctioned sphere where citizens can talk and perform while not being the object of state infringement. In this sphere a citizen is off duty. The police has to respect the privacy of the citizen's home. A raid can not be performed before 6 am. Therefore, it is not surprising to see protests and critique against the invasion of privacy by the state.

Citizen Rights and AK Vorrat

When 34,000 German citizens sued their government for the implemen-tation of the European data retention scheme on the last day of the year 2007, this was regarded as a major hallmark of a new pro-privacy movement. The Arbeitskreis Vorratsdatenspeicherung (AK Vorrat) used the Internet as a major organizing tool from the beginning, making it easy to join in. This has been branded 'activism 2.0' with reference to Web 2.0. The AK Vorrat can be described as an alliance or network of individuals, NGOs rooted in humanism or liberalism and a decent amount of lawyers were eager from the start to prove that data retention does not comply with the constitution. Professionals in

IT, mostly connected with the Chaos Computer Club, also played an important role, offering technological know-how to criticise, among other things, the possible 'abuse' of data.

This coalition has had a considerable impact on the discourse on data retention. Journalists, themselves not exempted from data retention (unlike priests), cooperated as well.

On 22 January 2007, AK Vorrat had already published an appeal to politicians to let go of the complete data retention idea. It was signed by 50 organizations, among them the German league for human rights, the international league for human rights and Reporters Without Borders.

Wolfgang Schäuble, the minister of the interior at the time, was not officially responsible for the law proposal, but was seen as one of the driving forces behind it. He and his first secretary August Hanning, former head of the BND (federal German secret service), resented the criticism and delegated the issue to the courts, which are to decide if the law passed by the legislative violates constitutional rights or not.

The Appeal to the Judiciary

The appeal to the judiciary by both politicians and protesters is of importance to understand the nature of this protest movement and the nature of contemporary politics. It has become a common procedure in Germany for new laws to be approved or rejected by the federal courts. The court as a touchstone and adviser on how to legislate indicates the erosion of the liberal state in itself. Whereas an excess of executive power has become a common phenomena in most liberal democratic countries, excess of the legislative power by instrumentalizing the judiciary points towards a non-institutional unification of all three powers.

So interestingly, both protesters and politicians seem to agree with each other in addressing the judiciary, those who rule over what a law can be and what not. The politicians will learn what to change to make data retention compliant to the constitution. In their worst-case scenario, the court will reject the surveillance program *in toto*. But historically, the court has usually provided suggestions on how a law can be made compliant with the constitution or even on what part of the constitution needs to be changed to allow the law. In doing so, the judiciary promotes the blurring of powers.

The protest movement has aimed at going to court from the beginning, portraying the judiciary as an independent power. In some statements by some lawyers of AK Vorrat the idea of data retention is not rejected completely. It is argued it might help to prevent crime and terrorism. They therefore differentiate between good citizens, whose rights are under threat, and the bad outcasts, who do not seem to have the same rights. The Privacy 2.0 movements' cornerstone is its positive relation to the state. It is not an anarchist movement, neither does it show any leftist ambitions. It is not about solidarity with migrants or the working poor, it is not about neoliberal agendas or free trade of services. But the fight for the right to privacy cannot be a single-issue movement, as privacy and the loss of it have wide-ranging consequences.

Data Retention and Post-Fordist Labour

When Paolo Virno identified the post-Fordist labour condition by referring to Marx's notion of the General Intellect, as leading to the 'communism of capital', he referred to new qualities, such as communication and socialization skills, as necessities for the post-Fordist worker. In short, capital was able to integrate and valorise qualities that had emerged among the social movements of the 1970s and '80s in Italy. Post-Fordism, a counterrevolutionary strategy according to Virno, reduces more and more aspects of life to work. But Virno is clear in that capital is always at risk of not being fully able to integrate all aspects of the communication potentialities of the multitude[2] while at the same time capital needs to take full advantage of electronic communications as a means of generating surplus value. The data retention scheme is structured to satisfy both the need of control and that of communicative production. Protesting the advent of data retention is a fight for the commons of communications versus the attempts to enclose, commodify and restructure them under present historical circumstances, where the General Intellect is as important to capital as fixed capital was before.

2. The multitude is an abstract term, a similitude of the working class. Besides that, it contains far more potentiality than the latter, as it stems from forms of life and not from commodity production. See Paolo Virno, *A Grammar of the Multitude: For an Analysis of Contemporary Forms of Life* (New York: Semiotext(e), 2004).

The Good Citizen and the Bad Militant

With the arrest and detention of sociologist Andrej Holm as part of a § 129a investigation by the feds in Germany on 31 July 2007, an interesting observation could be made with regard to AK Vorrat.

In Germany, law enforcements' legal means for infiltrating, surveilling and detaining political opponents have been steadily extended and increasingly enforced since the 1970s. The most prominent case is § 129 of the criminal code, dealing with criminal organizations and its 'big brothers' § 129a (terrorists organizations) plus § 129b (foreign terrorist organizations). These laws are basically stripping suspects from every last bit of their rights and have been used mostly by law enforcement to update their knowledge on leftist activists. Hardly any of the numerous 129a investigations made it to court. More than 90 per cent were silently shut down when enough information was gathered. Interestingly, the number of cases targeting the extreme right is almost zero.

So, Andrej Holm was (and is!) subject to obsessive surveillance, including his partner and children, and his huge social network. He was arrested under the suspicion of membership of a phantom-like militant group, funnily enough going under the same name: 'militante gruppe'. But not only Andrej was arrested. Along with him three other suspects were locked behind bars and stayed there much longer than he did.

By blogging about her everyday life as a partner of a suspected terrorist, Anne Roth (Holm's partner) for the first time gave insights into what so far has been the exclusive knowledge or experience of the radical left: a life completely under surveillance, the experience of a temporal totalitarianism so to speak. By using the Internet to mobilize the netizens and bloggers, Anne Roth made the case valuable for the media sphere. Fittingly, public awareness about the case was produced with the exact communication means that are under threat by data retention: Internet communication. She reported the latest disclosed surveillance measure, started inquiries about her phone that functioned strangely, mobilized hackers for expertise, and reached a large audience, including journalists from newspapers, radio and television. This led to a huge public interest in the wellbeing of Andrej but not in the wellbeing of any other person prosecuted under 129, 129a or b.

Why not? Because Andrej proved to have enough qualities to be regarded as a citizen, whereas most of the other suspects lacked the appeal to be seen as such. AK Vorrat regarded Andrej as a case of a good citizen who was mistaken for a terrorist, AK Vorrat helped to separate the black from the white sheep, the good citizen from the outcasts, even prior to any court ruling against the accused. In neglecting the principle of Habeas Corpus, AK Vorrat showed a strange disregard towards the liberal principles it is fighting for. Being concerned with preserving the clean image of the good, innocent citizen who protests for his or her legitimate rights, it missed out on another important part of its role: to fight detention without verdict.

Post-Fordist Privacy

Privacy has become one of the central issues of the current organi-zation of capital and labour, as it is a means (among other things) to nurture the chatter of the multitude to come. Privacy can not be stripped of its relevance to the political economy, as post-Fordist labour is centred on communication and information. Once the privacy movement relates their trajectories to the current labour situ-ation, an important, so far missing element would be brought into the political reflections on the multitude.

Martijn de Waal

New Use of Cellular Networks

The Necessity of Recognizing

the Nuances of Privacy

According to media researcher Martijn de Waal, it is time to rethink our ideas of privacy. The growing use of cellular networks is generating data that plays an important role in civil society projects. To be able to continue using such data in a meaningful and fair way, people must become aware of the fact that privacy is not only a question of either private or public, but includes many gradations in between.

During the Notte Bianca 2007 (an event in Rome comparable with the Museum Night in the Netherlands), researchers from MIT's SENSEable City Lab set up at different urban locations a number of big screens upon which they projected dynamic maps of the city. Light blue spots indicated large numbers of people, thus enabling visitors to the event to immediately see which museum was crowded and plan their route accordingly. Making the task even easier, yellow stripes representing Rome's municipal buses could be followed live on the same map. This project – 'WikiCity Rome' – sounds like a nice gimmick. The researchers gained access to the location data of mobile phone users through a telecom company. The anonymized coordinates of individual phones were combined to compile an algorithm of a – handsomely designed – real-time map of nighttime Rome.[1]

1. See: senseable.mit.edu/wikicity/rome/ for a summary of the project and, for an extensive analysis of the project, Francesco Calabrese, Kristian Kloeckl and Carlo Ratti, 'WikiCity: Real-Time Location-Sensitive Tools for the City', in: Marcus Foth (ed.), *Handbook of Research on Urban Informatics: The Practice and Promise of the Real-Time City* (London/Hershey, PA: Information Science Reference, 2009).

But 'WikiCity Rome' was more than just a gimmick. The project made use of an important shift in the functionality of the mobile phone (or 'cellphone', as it is called in parts of the English-speaking world). It is no longer simply a means of communication. Increasingly, the mobile phone is also being used as a sensor that gathers information about us and our surroundings.[2] Location coordinates, images and sounds can be recorded and shared with friends, colleagues, social institutes or even with others who are unknown to us. This new use of mobile phones can have great social consequences, but it also raises questions about privacy. Who has access to all of this data we are gathering? To whom does this information actually belong? To us? The telephone company? Or should it – in anonymous form of course – be considered common property? Ought the government be allowed to monitor our movements in times of emergency? And if so, precisely what constitutes an emergency?

2. For example, see Eric Paulos, who maintains that there is an 'important new shift in mobile phone usage – from communication tool to "networked mobile personal measurement instrument"'. Eric Paulos, 'Designing for Doubt: Citizen Science and the Challenge of Change', lecture for the conference 'Engaging Data', Cambridge, MA: SENSEable City Lab, 2009. http://senseable.mit.edu/engagingdata/program.html

For the American civil rights organization Electronic Frontier Foundation (EFF), these developments are sufficient reason to introduce a new category of privacy: 'locational privacy'. Will we still be able to move through a city in the near future without the places we go to being systematically recorded in all sorts of databases?[3] The new developments are so far-reaching that we must ask ourselves whether our traditional idea of privacy is still tenable. The discussion is no longer only about the right to be able to act anonymously in our private lives without the government or our employers looking over our shoulders. In many instances, people will actually want to voluntarily make information

3. www.eff.org/wp/locational-privacy.

about their private lives public. For the fact of the matter is that this can also have certain advantages, both for individuals and for society as a whole. But precisely what are the conditions under which this occurs? What possibilities does technology offer for sharing or protecting information? In this essay, I would first like to give a number of examples of how the use of the mobile phone as a sensor encroaches upon our lives in today's society. Then I will go into the consequences of this for the debate on privacy and technology.

Scientific Research: A New Form of Demography?

Researchers in various disciplines are extremely enthusiastic about the mobile phone as a means of collecting data. Finally, they sigh, we can chart the behaviour of an entire population in real time instead of taking a few random samples afterwards. 'Reality Mining' is the name of the new discipline in which different streams of data are combined to get a handle on complex social processes. Social scientists often speak in slightly euphoric terms about these new possibilities. For instance, take Alex Pentland of the MIT Medialab: 'By using data from mobile phones . . . we can create a "god's eye" view of how the people in organizations interact, and even "see" the rhythms of interaction for everyone in a city.'[4] This new method of measuring not only gives better insight into social processes, claims Pentland, it also has greater predictive value. Traditional demography, he states, is   4. web.media.mit.edu/~sandy/.
a bad predictor of behaviour. How old someone is, where they live and even their income is interesting information, but says little about how that person will behave in the future. Only when you can actually analyse their behaviour, can you – within certain margins – start predicting. Says Pentland: 'The fact that mobile phones have GPS means that we can leap beyond demographics directly to measuring behaviour. Where do people eat? Work? Hang out?

How does word of mouth spread? Analysis of travel patterns using mobile phone GPS data, for instance, allows discovery of the independent subgroups within a city.'[5]

5. Alex Pentland, 'Reality Mining of Mobile Communications', *The Global Information Technology Report 2008-2009*. World Economic Forum, 2009.

At present, the mobile phone is already being used in this manner for health care research. In Kenya, for example, mobile phone data is being used to localize breeding grounds of infection for malaria. Other scientists have developed algorithms with which – again through data generated by mobile phone use – behavioural patterns that indicate the outbreak of a cholera epidemic can be identified. In the Dominican Republic, research into the spread of HIV is being conducted in a similar fashion.[6]

6. See Nathan Eagle, 'Engineering a Common Good: Fair Use of Aggregated, Anonymized Behavioral Data', lecture for the conference 'Engaging Data', Cambridge, MA: SENSEable City Lab, 2009.

Urban planners are also enthusiastic about this new way of collecting information. The British 'Cityware' project tracked visitors to inner cities with the help of the Bluetooth technology on their phones.[7] Here too, expectations are often high. Anthony Townsend, for instance, a researcher specialized in technology, sees the rise of   7. www.cityware.org.uk. networked sensors as a development comparable to the rise of aerial photography. For urban planners, that was a revolutionary media technology: for the first time, they could see the city from above, as a whole. And if aerial photography reveals the city's skeleton, we now have a view of its nervous system. For the first time in history, people often optimistically say, we can observe all sorts of social interactions in the city in real time.

A little perspective is not out of place here, however. Although these methods of gathering data certainly can lead to new insights, the debate still does not address the question of exactly what kind of knowledge they actually produce. Data is not the same as knowledge, and so far the nature of the data is primarily quantitative. Researchers now know how many people are at certain places at certain times, where they have come from and where they are going. But more qualitative aspects – why do people move as they do, and what is their experience of that? – still remain out of the picture as a rule.

Citizen Science

In the above instances, scientists work from the top down in collecting great amounts of data in order to analyse social processes. But the mobile phone can also be used to collect data from the bottom up, at the initiative of users themselves. 'Biketastic', a project aimed at bicyclists in the notoriously car-oriented city of Los Angeles that has been set up by the Center for Embedded Networked Sensing, is one such example. This research centre from the University of California Los Angeles has developed a mobile phone app that bicyclists can use to collect data on their trips through the city and share it with one another. The app measures the location, distance and speed of the bicycle route, but also its comfort. The microphone measures the noise of the other traffic, while the accelerometer indicates whether the cyclist can smoothly cruise along or has to keep stopping and starting. The geographical data can later be linked with external databases: How much air pollution is there throughout the route? And what about traffic safety? By combining the data from different cyclists with external databases, after a while you also get a bicycle map of Los Angeles with which you can plan the most pleasant, safest, cleanest or fastest route.[8]

This is similar to a number of 'Citizen Science' projects, in which citizens use the mobile phone's sensor capacity in   8. See: research.cens.ucla.edu and order to work together for a specific purpose.   http://biketastic.com/.

Eric Paulos conducted research on campaigns in which neighbourhood residents charted the quality of the air with the help of mobile sensors. Such campaigns had many positive effects. The participants gained an increased awareness of the problem of air quality and their involvement in local politics improved.[9] But there are also negative aspects: Just how trustworthy is the data that is collected? Can the results be influenced, for example by holding a sensor next to a car muffler?[10]

9. Paulos, 'Designing for Doubt', op. cit. (note 2). Also see Jason Corburn, *Street Science: Community Knowledge and Environmental Health Justice* (Cambridge, MA: MIT Press, 2005).

10. Paulos, 'Designing for Doubt', ibid.

Personalized Locational Services

Finally, the use of the mobile phone as a sensor can also have advantages for individual users. The mobile phone makes it possible to register information about your life automatically. Services like Google Latitude or Bliin plot your movements through the city on a map. You yourself are always at the centre, surrounded by those of your friends who have the service turned on and voluntarily share their data with you. Other services, like Yelp in the USA, also centre the map on the user's position and then place balloon markers for the nearest pizzeria, optician, cash dispenser, taxi or other search command. Companies like Sensenetworks can also make analyses of your spatial behaviour and use that to recommend all sorts of services to you.

Christophe Aguiton, Dominique Cardon and Zbigniew Smoreda – researchers at Orange Labs, the R&D department of France Telecom – call this phenomenon 'Living Maps'. A map is no longer a static representation of a geographical reality but a dynamic reflection of social activities. In the long run, the advent of such maps can lead to a cultural shift. Right now, our social lives still largely consist of making appointments that we write down in our agendas. But after a while, a 'map of opportunities' might very well seem like a much more attractive idea. If you momentarily have nothing to do, simply take a look at your personalized map. Who is in the immediate vicinity right now to meet up with? What is there to do at a reasonable distance from where I am?[11]

Critics point out that this can have huge consequences for life in the city. Does it still leave any room for chance encounters with the unknown? Will we become 'people without characteristic traits' who slavishly follow the

11. Christophe Aguiton, Dominique Cardon and Zbigniew Smoreda, 'Living Maps: New Data, New Uses, New Problems', lecture for the conference 'Engaging Data', Cambridge, MA: SENSEable City Lab, 2009. Also see recent lectures by Antoine Picon and Nanna Verhoeff, in which they respectively describe how digital maps can be understood as 'media events' or 'performance of space' instead of only a 'systematic geographic representation'. http://www.themobilecity.nl/2008/01/22/mediacity-conference-weimar-the-design-of-urban-situations/ and http://networkcultures.org/wpmu/urbanscreens/2009/12/05/nanna-verhoeff-mobile-digital-cartography-from-representation-to-performance-of-space/.

recommendations of our 'clever' systems? These are relevant and meaningful discussions, which I do not wish to go into further right now. In the second part of this essay, I prefer to examine the notion of privacy that is at stake with these new technologies.[12]

12. See, among others, Mark Shepard and Adam Greenfield, *Urban Computing and Its Discontents* (New York: The Architectural League of New York, 2007); Jerome E. Dobson and Peter Fischer, 'Geoslavery', in: *IEEE Technology and Society Magazine*, Spring 2003.

Who Is the Owner?

How does the advent of the mobile phone as a sensor relate to our thinking about privacy? In academic circles, a cautious consensus is becoming apparent: users should be the owners of their own data. No matter how you generate data – for example, through the sensors in your mobile phone – you must be able to access that data, wipe it out yourself, keep it saved securely, and decide what is going to happen with it. Only in very exceptional circumstances should the government be able to have access to such databases.[13] A view like this could very well lead to new forms of inequality. Personal particulars are very attrac-

13. Pentland, op. cit. (note 5).

tive data for commercial parties, and some critics suspect that the selling of your personal data will be made attractive. People who don't want to share their personal details with commercial parties will, for example, have to pay more for a mobile phone subscription.[14]

14. Eagle, 'Engineering a Common Good', op. cit. (note 6).

Precisely what does 'data ownership' mean for the analysis of information on an aggregated scale? Are researchers only allowed to collect data if phone users give them permission to do so? And is that permission also necessary if the data is only used for mapping group behaviour? After all, in such cases the individual information is swallowed up in the group profile and a link with individual behaviour can no longer be made. But then, who is allowed to collect this sort of information, and under what conditions? Should telephone companies collaborate on this, for example?

Erin Keneally and Kimberly Claffy – researchers at UC San Diego – argue in favour of regulation that takes into account the positive aspects of sharing data. At present, the rules are not always so clear about what is allowed and what is not. As a result, many parties react defensively to requests for sharing data. They prefer not to take risks, seeing as the debate on privacy escalates quickly. The idea of privacy as the absolute right to protection of personal particulars soon loses out to the possible social benefits of sharing data – such as in the above-mentioned instances in the area of health care, for example. Keneally and Claffy call upon researchers and the telecom industry to develop a new protocol that makes the sharing of data possible and at the same time limits the risks of improper use of sensitive information.

Nathan Eagle compares 'reality mining' with large-scale medical research projects. There too, extremely sensitive personal information is stored in databases, which is why there are strict rules for their use: only professionals have access to the information and they must sign in when they want to use the databases. Eagle therefore proposes that such protocols also be quickly set up for the use of sensor data from mobile phones.

Organizations like the Dutch 'Bits of Freedom' are concerned about these new developments. Information that is stored anonymously, warns this organization, does not always remain that way. 'Better technologies are always being developed to strip anonymous data of their anonymity. What might not be a "personal detail" now can soon turn into one.'[15] Researchers Aguiton, Cardon and Smoreda concur. More than once in the past, new technologies have made it possible to trace anonymous data to specific users.[16]

15. www.bof.nl/2009/12/18/hoe-anoniem-zijn-anonieme-gegevens-eigenlijk/.

16. Aguiton et al, 'Living Maps', op. cit. (note 11).

The EFF therefore proposes using cryptography to design systems such that sensor information can be used without having to store it. Technologically, this is a rather roundabout way, although possible: 'But we need to ensure that systems aren't being built right at the zero-privacy, everything-is-recorded end of that spectrum, simply because that's the path of easiest implementation.'[17]

17. www.eff.org/wp/locational-privacy.

The Desire to Share Data

The EFF's idea of using strong cryptography can protect personal sensor data. That might come in handy with a system like pay-as-you-drive, for example. But there are also situations in which users do want to share their data, albeit not necessarily always or with everyone.

In daily life, privacy is a complex and above all dynamic negotiation between various parties, argue researchers Paul Dourish and Leysia Palen. In social situations, what plays a role is not so much the fear of the state's misusing information but is much more likely to be ordinary worries. People do not want to be embarrassed. They want to assert their authority or voice in a certain area. And they like to have control over their own lives. Because of this, we make different demands of privacy at different moments.

In social situations it is often more important to make yourself known than to protect your privacy. If you want to capitalize on your authority in a certain area, you have to be able to show the corresponding badges. With the help of all sorts of signs – varying from word choice to greeting rituals – we send out signals through which others can deduce our social status or background. Sometimes we want to give our opinion, or we benefit from letting others know who we are. Just how much we wish to reveal depends upon what estimate we make of a situation. Who exactly is the audience? What do we expect, hope or fear in regard to the situation? Privacy, in other words, is a question of 'identity management', in which we show or conceal different aspects of ourselves to different audiences in different situations.

Palen and Dourish's most important point is that the use of the mobile phone as a sensor, combined with the storage of information in databases, changes the parameters of this privacy negotiation. The situations in which we find ourselves are originally spatial and temporal. They are physically limited, for instance by the four walls of a room, and have a certain duration. Both factors play an important role in the estimates we make. We can see who is present and who is not – and therefore who could call us to account for an eventual faux pas.

When we use automatic sensors to register our behaviour in all sorts of situations and share it with others – for instance through social networks – the nature of the situation changes. Suddenly, space, time and audience are no longer limited, and instead the registration of the situation can also be called up at other times and places. But can another audience actually interpret the original context of the situation properly? And maybe you would have acted very differently if you knew that the audience was going to be wider.

Researcher Danah Boyd has written about how this development can lead to all sorts of misunderstandings. As an expert on social networking, Boyd was approached by the admissions committee of a leading university. They had received an application from a student from South Central LA. In a letter describing his motivation, he wrote that he wanted to break away from the gang life there. But when the committee looked at his page on a social network, Myspace, they saw all sorts of symbols glorifying gang life. Was he making a fool of them? Boyd pointed out to the committee that there was also another possibility. The applicant's Myspace page was intended for his classmates and neighbours, not the admissions committee. And in his neighbourhood the social pressure to be part of something is so high that the young man probably could do nothing else but post the gang's insignia on his Myspace page.[18]

18. Danah Boyd, 'Do you See What I See? Visibility of Practices through Social Media', *LeWeb*, Paris, 2009.

Similarly, a commotion arose over the Facebook website. There too, users can voluntarily keep a log of their activities, hobbies and other titbits of information. At first this was only possible on the person's own page. But one day Facebook changed the setup of its site. All of the messages that users placed on their own page were now automatically published on the pages of all their 'friends'. Facebook's reasoning was that this way, friends would be better able to keep abreast of each other's activities. Besides, hadn't the information already been made public by users on their own page?

Facebook didn't do much more than publishing what was already public. But many Facebook users thought otherwise. They saw a subtle difference between making something public on one's own page, which others must make an effort to access, and automatically distributing that data.[19] Once again, this was about the assessment that users make of their audience in determining what information they do or do not wish to make public. To be sure, the information was now being distributed among friends, but there were also subtle diffe-rences within that. Some friends might very well be difficult co-workers that a person would not want to offend by rejecting their 'friendship request'. And people show different things to members of their family than they do to old school friends. Facebook does not make it possible to make that distinction.

19. Danah Boyd, 'Facebook's Privacy Trainwreck: Exposure, Invasion, and Social Convergence', in: *Convergence*, vol.14 (2008) no. 1, 13-20.

Privacy as Design Criterion

At the Center for Embedded Networked Sensing (CENS, the research lab behind the earlier-mentioned bicycle project in LA) they therefore believe that privacy is an important responsibility for designers. There should be a system that gives users the possibility to decide for themselves what information they want to share with whom, under what conditions, and for what length of time.[20] This is why it is important that designers develop systems that visualize information in an under-standable way and that immediately make it clear what sort of consequences certain settings can have.

20. Katie Shilton, 'Four Billion Little Brothers? Privacy, Mobile Phones, and Ubiquitous Data Collection', in: *Queue*, vol. 7 (2009) no. 7.

CENS itself uses such an application in its Personal Environmental Impact Report (PEIR) project, in which data is again collected with the help of mobile phones. This information is then converted into a carbon footprint and simultaneously combined with databases on local air pollu-tion. In this way, users not only learn how much they themselves contri-bute to air pollution but also how much pollution they are being exposed to. In a log file, users can see precisely how the system uses their data: what information is registered when, and uploaded and shared with whom. Eric Paulos argues that interfaces like this should also make clear how reliable such (collectively gathered) data are. It is important that users do not trust all flows of data blindly, but that they always remain aware that data can be manipulated, or even simply not collected accurately.[21]

Aguiton et al go one step further. Not only should users be able to have insight into the manner in which information about them is collected, they should also be able to manipulate that information. Users have the right to lie to the system about their actual whereabouts in order to protect their privacy, they claim.[22]

21. Paulos, 'Designing for Doubt', op. cit. (note 2).

22. Aguiton et al, 'Living Maps', op. cit. (note 11).

The above-mentioned examples show that our thinking about privacy has to be reconsidered. The sensor data collected by mobile phones can play an important social role, for example in the area of public health. Such data can – as in the 'citizen science' instances – play a role in civil society projects. And some people will experience sharing data with others as an enrichment of their lives.

Involved parties point out that many of the present regulations are inadequate. On the one hand, the positive aspects of sharing data anonymously should be given more attention. At the same time, the awareness must also grow that privacy is not a binary affair in which something is either completely public or completely private. Between the two extremes lie many gradations that by no means are always taken into consideration in the design of new technologies. And providers of location services and social networks, for example, should also be stimulated to give the many nuances of privacy in everyday life a place in their services.

Mark Shepard

Near-Future Urban Archaeology

The Sentient City Survival Kit

To what extent can artists and designers develop instruments that, using the newest digital technology, question how we will live our lives in the (near) future? In search of an answer, the editors of *Open* asked artist, architect and researcher Mark Shepard to write about his research project The Sentient City Survival Kit.

The Sentient City Survival Kit is a design research project that probes the social, cultural and political implications of ubiquitous computing for urban environments. Conceived as an archaeology of the near future, the project consists of designing, fabricating and publicly presenting a collection of artefacts for 'survival' in the near-future 'sentient' city.

As computing leaves the desktop and spills out onto the sidewalks, streets and public spaces of the city, information processing becomes embedded in and distributed throughout the material fabric of everyday urban space. Ubiquitous computing evangelists herald a coming age of urban information systems capable of sensing and responding to the events and activities transpiring around them. Imbued with the capacity to remember, correlate and anticipate, this 'sentient' city is envisioned as being capable of reflexively monitoring our behaviour within it and becoming an active agent in the organization of our daily lives.

Few may quibble about 'smart' traffic light control systems that more efficiently manage the ebbs and flows of trucks, cars and busses on our city streets. Some may be irritated when discount coupons for their favourite espresso drink are beamed to their mobile phone as they pass by Starbucks. Many are likely to protest when they are denied passage through a subway turnstile because the system 'senses' that their purchasing habits, mobility patterns and current galvanic skin response (GSR) reading happens to match the profile of a terrorist.

The project investigates the darker side of this near future urban imaginary and posits a set of playful and ironic technosocial artefacts that explore the implications for privacy, autonomy, trust and serendipity of this highly observant, ever more efficient and overcoded city.

Context-awareness plays a significant role in current research in sentient systems. In addition to sensing where someone is, factors such as whom they are with and what time of day it is reduces the possibility space within which inferences and predictions are made. This real-time information is correlated with historical data of someone's mobility patterns, purchasing history, social relations and personal preferences (as reflected by user-generated profiles) in order to make more accurate predictions about what his or her wants and needs may currently be, or what actions s/he is likely to take next.

MIT's Serendipity project,[1] for example, draws on the real-time sensing of proximate others using Bluetooth technologies built into mobile phones to search for matching patterns in profiles of people's interests. Developed by the Human Dynamics Group at the Media Lab, the project's goal is to facilitate corporate productivity by providing a matchmaking service for workers with shared interests or complimentary needs and skills who otherwise might not encounter each other within spaces organized around the office cubicle. A typical design scenario involves one worker needing the skills of another and the system facilitating their meeting: 'When we were passing each other in the hallway, my phone would sense the presence of his phone. It would then connect to our server, which would recognize that Tom has extensive expertise in a specific area that I was currently struggling with. If both of our phones had been set to "available" mode, two picture messages would have been sent to alert us of our common interests, and we might have stopped to talk instead of walking by each other.'[2]

1. http://reality.media.mit.edu/serendipity.php.

2. See Nathan Eagle, 'Can Serendipity Be Planned?', *MIT Sloan Management Review*, vol. 46 (2004) no. 1, 10-14.

This project presents at least two assumptions that are worth exploring further. The first is that 'matchmaking' should be based on comparing profiles and looking for 'synergies' between two people. If the term 'serendipity' is understood to mean the process of finding something by looking for something else, the Serendipity project does precisely the opposite: it simply outsources the problem of finding something we are already looking for (that 'expertise in a specific area that I was currently struggling with' that I have somehow indicated in my profile). Secondly, while the introduction of 'available' mode suggests that some attempt has been made to address privacy issues, there is no consideration of who has access to your profile data and how they use it.

Profile data considered private in one context can be publicly revealing in another. A another MIT project by two graduate students, code-named *Gaydar*,[3] mined Facebook profile information to see if people were revealing more than they realized by using the social networking site. By looking at a person's on-line friends, they found that they could predict that person's sexual orientation. They did this with a software program that looked at the gender and sexuality of a person's friends and, using statistical analysis, made a prediction. While the project lacked scientific rigor – they verified their results using their personal knowledge of 10 people in the network who were gay but did not declare it on their Facebook page – it does point to the possibility that information disclosed in one context may be used to interpret information in another.

3. abcnews.go.com/Technology/gaydar-facebook-friends/story?id=8633224.

Crang and Graham's recent essay 'Sentient Cities: Ambient Intelligence and the Politics of Urban Space'[4] does a great job at outlining how corporate and military agendas are currently driving these technological ecosystems we're likely to cohabit with in the near future. Mapping current research and development on the Sentient City, they point to location-based search results and target-marketing databases storing finely grained purchasing histories as steps toward 'data-driven mass customization based on continuous, real-time monitoring of consumers'. Further, citing a study by the US Defense Science Board calling for a 'New Manhattan Project' based on Ambient Intelligence for 'Tracking, Targeting and Locating' they outline an Orwellian future that is in fact currently in operation in lower Manhattan.

4. See Mike Crang and Stephen Graham, 'Sentient Cities: Ambient Intelligence and the Politics of Urban Space', *Information, Communication & Society*, vol. 10 (2007) no. 6, 789-817.

The Lower Manhattan Security Initiative,[5] as the plan is called, resembles London's so-called Ring of Steel, an extensive web of cameras and roadblocks designed to detect, track and deter terrorists. The system went live in November 2008 with 156 surveillance cameras and 30 mobile license plate readers. Designed for 3,000 public and private security cameras below Canal Street, this system will include not only license plate readers but also movable roadblocks. Pivoting gates would be installed at critical intersections and would swing out to block traffic or a suspect car at the push of a button.

5. www.nytimes.com/2007/07/09/nyregion/09ring.html.

While the implications of projects like *Serendipity* occupy a relatively benign problem space, *The Lower Manhattan Security Initiative* points towards possibly more serious outcomes from the false positives (or false negatives) inevitably generated by the pattern matching and data mining algorithms at the core of these systems. What happens when Facebook profile data is added to the mix? Is information about us that is collected through inference engines subject to the same privacy regulations as the data upon which it is based? What are the mechanisms by which these systems will gain our trust? In what ways does our autonomy become compromised? Do we care and does it matter? How do the answers to these questions differ depending upon where in the world they are asked?

While it may be intriguing to attempt to pose answers to these speculative questions about potential futures, perhaps a more pressing challenge is to identify concrete examples in the present around which we might organize a public debate that aims to both sharpen and broaden the questions we ask ourselves about what kind of future we want. In the wake of a massive, global financial crisis and increasingly grim environmental forecasts, the general public is finally beginning to register that as a planet we need to negotiate our way of life with those of the various actants and ecosystems with which we cohabitate, be they environmental, political, economic, social or technological. While Crang and Graham do help us understand current corporate and military agendas, their analysis of the role of artists and designers working with embedded and pervasive technologies as one of 're-enchanting urban space' – of making visible the invisible traces of things past, a 'haunting of place with absent others' – renders artistic practice in relatively conservative and familiar terms, casting art in a reactionary role vis-à-vis technological development. What other roles might artists, architects and designers play in shaping how we inhabit the near-future Sentient City?

The Sentient City Survival Kit takes as its method a critical design practice that looks towards archaeology for guidance. Archaeology involves the (re)construction of a world through fragments of artefacts, where past cultures are reconstituted in the present through specific socializing and spatializing practices involving mapping, classifying, collecting and curating. Cultural knowledge is reproduced through relating in space and time the traces and remains of people, places, things, activities and events. Collections of archaeological artefacts serve to reveal the everyday social and spatial relations of societies not contemporary with ours, yet recontextualized within the present. Greg Stevenson refers to an archaeology of the contemporary past as 'the design history of the everyday',[6] where common objects drawn from daily life do not simply (passively) reflect cultural forces (trends in taste and fashion, for example) but also actively participate in shaping the evolving social and spatial relations between people and their environment.

6. See Greg Stevenson, 'Archaeology as the Design History of the Everyday, in: V. Buchli and G. Lucas (eds.), *Archaeology of the Contemporary Past* (London: Routledge, 2001), 53.

Positing an archaeology not of the contemporary past but of the proximate future, the project takes the practice of designing everyday artefacts as a vehicle for shaping tomorrow's cities. The aim here is to attempt to instigate the process of imagining a future city and its inhabitants through fragments and traces of a society yet to exist. Collectively, the artefacts, spaces and media that constitute the Survival Kit ask: Who made me, and for what purpose? What relations between people and their environment do I suggest? In what places, circumstances and situations would I be found? In what kind of city would I be viable, useful, necessary, or even popular?

Ultimately the project is less invested in forecasting future trends in technology than focused on provoking public discussion in the present about just what kind of future we might want. This involves a design process based on looking at what's happening just upstream in the computer science and engineering R&D labs and teasing out some of the more absurd assumptions, latent biases and hidden agendas at play. The production of physical working prototypes for items in the Survival Kit subsequently involves playing out the design implications of these assumptions, biases and agendas.

Figure 1 - GPS Serendipitor

In the near future, finding our way from point A to point B will not be the problem. Maintaining consciousness of what happens along the way might be more difficult. The GPS Serendipitor is an alternative GPS navigation software application for mobile phones that determines a route to a destination that the user has not previously taken, designed to facilitate finding something by looking for something else.

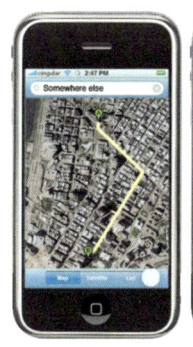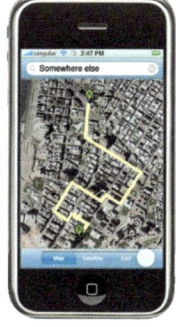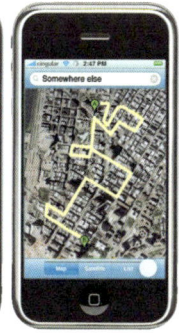

NAVIGATION ROUTE BASED ON MINIMUM TRAVEL DISTANCE

ALTERNATE ROUTE BASED ON STREETS NOT YET WALKED (BEGINNER)

ALTERNATE ROUTE BASED ON STREETS NOT YET WALKED (ADVANCED)

Figure 2 - RFID under(a)ware

In the near-future sentient shopping centre, item-level tagging and discrete data-sniffing are both common corporate culture and popular criminal activities. This popular product line consists of his and her underwear designed to sense hidden Radio Frequency Identification (RFID) Tag readers, alert the wearer to their presence, and make the whole affair a pleasurable experience by activating small vibrators sewn into bras and boxer shorts in strategic locations.

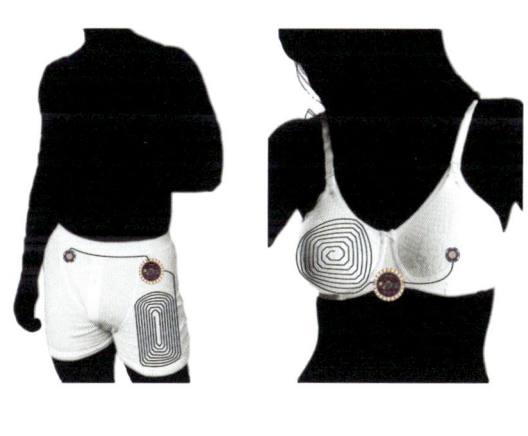

 + 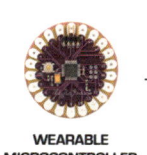 +

WEARABLE VIBE BOARD

WEARABLE MICROCONTROLLER

CONDUCTIVE THREAD

Figure 3 - Ad-hoc Dark (roast) Travel Mug

In an environment where all network traffic is monitored via 'smart' filters, where access privileges are dynamically granted and denied on the fly based on your credit card transaction history, and where bandwidth is a function of your market capitalization, standard commuter gear includes this travel mug designed for creating ad-hoc 'dark' networks for communication along a morning commute. Caffeinated commuters share short messages tapped out in Morse code on the side of the mug and picked up by a capacitance sensor.

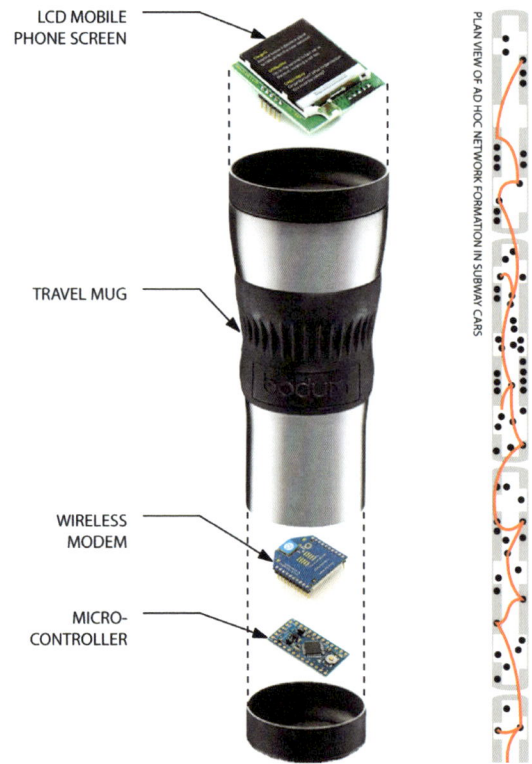

LCD MOBILE PHONE SCREEN

TRAVEL MUG

WIRELESS MODEM

MICRO-CONTROLLER

PLAN VIEW OF AD-HOC NETWORK FORMATION IN SUBWAY CARS

Anyone know a discrete place to talk about opposition to the new national identity card proposal?

Don't work for Google. They share the biometric data they capture for new employees with the NSA!

www.whatreallyhappened.com

Figure 4 - CCD-me-not Umbrella
When human vision is no longer
the only game in town, don't
leave home without this umbrella studded with infrared
LEDs visible only to CCD surveillance cameras, designed
to frustrate object detection
algorithms used in computer vision surveillance systems. Use
in pairs with a friend to train
these systems to recognize non-
human shapes and patterns more
common to dreams and hallucina-
tions than to your average city
street

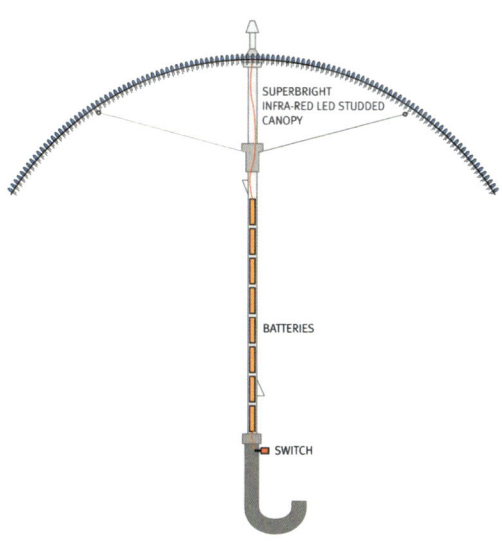

Rob van Kranenburg

From Privacy to Privacies

Rob van Kranenburg explores the field of the Internet of Things and is founder of the think-tank 'Council'.[1] With regard to the infrastructure of technologies and networks that connect us with one another and our environment, he argues in favour of making concepts of privacy operational from the bottom up. Only then can we free ourselves from the primacy of the security mentality.

1. Rob van Kranenburg, *The Internet of Things. A critique of ambient technology and the all-seeing network of RFID*, Network Notebook no. 2 (Amsterdam: Institute of Network Cultures, 2008). For Council, see: http://www.theinternetofthings.eu.

'I was taught to talk to the plants and tell them what I need them for.'[2]

2. From the poem *Paiute Native American Shaman Wovoka and the Ghost Dance* by Judy Trejo (see You Tube).

In the twenty-first century, identity is evolving into a changing constellation of relations between a person, his or her things and an 'intelligent' environment. All of today's computer paradigms focus on connectivity: the Internet of Things, Pervasive Computing, Ubiquitous Computing and Ambient Intelligence are every one of them concepts denoting an environment that functions as an interface, and in which people, computers, the Internet and objects jointly and severally form networks. This is developing very rapidly at the moment. In 1991, scientist Mark Weiser, the 'Father of Ubiquitous Computing', instigated a new way of thinking about computers – not to make them even faster and more intelligent, but to provide the environment itself with connectivity and reactive capacity.[3] In the late 1990s, two factors caused a breakthrough in this area: the steadily dropping prices of radio frequency identification (RFID) tags, with which objects can be identified through a unique code – something that is conceivable for all objects – and of data storage capacity.

3. Mark Weiser, 'The Computer for the 21st Century', *Scientific American*, September 1991.

The glue for this almost fairytale-like situation in which everything is connected to everything else is an ecosystem of RFID tags, active sensors, barcodes and cameras with all sorts of software, in combination with biometric data recognition. There is no turning back from this new ecology. With the Internet of Things, not only can 'things' be read with a special code, but our thinking about the Internet itself changes. Playing a big role in this is IPv6, the new protocol for sending data over the Internet. Whereas the present IPv4 is reaching the limits of its capacity (every computer or application on the Internet needs a unique Internet protocol – IP – number, and with the IPv4 system no more than 4 billion can be made, which nowadays also includes connections for mobile phones, refrigerators, automobiles and entire houses), IPv6 provides a large number of IP addresses for every square metre of the earth's surface. The following scenario then becomes reality: 'If a guest is charging their electric car at a friend's house, we should consider applications that will understand that the charge should appear on the guest's electric bill and not that of the friend.'[4]

4. Motivation for SIP as an application protocol for 6lowpan devices, draft-roychowdhury-6lowappsip-00 http://www.openremote.org/pages/viewpage.action?pageId=4948218.

In such an environment, in which the privacy of objects is just as relevant or irrelevant as the privacy of persons, it is not productive to maintain old constants. Rudolf Arnheim wrote in 1989: 'To be sure, computations such as those performed by electronic devices do not need to do their own perceiving. They produce mere combinations of items, to which meaning is attributed from the outside. A computation mechanism cannot tell the difference between airplane reservations, chess games or medical diagnoses. Thought processes worthy of the name go beyond mere computation. Inevitably, they rely on imagery, especially on vision.'[5] This subject-object approach, which forms the basis of the philosophical and ethical principles we always have taken as a guideline for our actions in a society, is no longer relevant in a world where the hallmark of computations made by electronic devices is that they actually do understand what they are doing.

5. Rudolf Arnheim, 'Thoughts on Art Education', *Occasional Paper 2* (Los Angeles: The J.P. Getty Trust, 1989), 16.

The fundamental problem now manifesting itself does not so much lie in the experience of identity fragmentation – with citizens integrating their physical surroundings with the Internet through the application Layar,[6] phoning to get real-time information from real estate agents, driving by the road-pricing system, carrying biometric passports and communicating through Twitter, Facebook, LinkedIn and Hyves – but in the concept of identity wielded by states and democratic institutes. For them, identity still entirely corresponds with the personal biometrical data of natural persons – with there being an identity that watches and an identity that is watched.

6. Layar, Browse The World! Mobile Augmented Reality Browser, http://layar.com/.

Security Dashboards and the Individual as Internal Security Issue

The Dutch independent research organization TNO and the University of Amsterdam participate in the European Union security project 'Automatic Detection of Abnormal Behaviour and Threats in Crowded Spaces (ADABTS)'. One of the key tasks of ADABTS is 'understanding of the user needs for automatic detection of abnormal behaviour in crowds and new definitions of and methods for describing such behaviour'.[7]

7. See: ftp://ftp.cordis.europa.eu/pub/fp7/security/.../adabts_en.pdf. Prepared by the European Committee, Directorate-General Enterprise and Industry, Unit H4 Security Research and Development, e-mail: entr-security-research@ec.europa.eu.

But who is the 'user' in this research? In another EU project, 'Changing Perceptions of Security and Interventions (CPSI)', TNO contact person Dr Heather J. Griffioen-Young states that the project is aimed at end-users, and that these are not citizens but government institutions at the local, provincial, national and international level, law enforcement agencies, emergency services, and other organizations that are involved in the development of policy and its implementation. With the CPSI methodology, it will be possible for these end-users to assess security all the way down to the neighbourhood level: 'The goal of the project is to provide governments and related organizations with a methodology to increase insight into the determinants of actual and perceived security, and into which interventions are effective for increasing security. The deliverables of this project represent practical and ready-to-use tools, which can be employed by policymakers and other end-users to formulate policy regarding security. In this project we will develop 1) a conceptual model of actual and perceived security and their determinants, 2) a methodology to collect, quantify, analyse and interpret security-related data, 3) a data warehouse to store and extract for analysis data amassed using the methodology, and 4) carry out a validation study to test the model, methodology and data warehouse. We will test if it is possible to answer relevant security-related questions from the field using the methodology. The project deliverables can be used by end-users to assess security at the international, national and local levels and to draw conclusions regarding such issues as: What are the levels of actual and perceived security in specific locations?, Which interventions work where?, and Which interventions should be implemented in which locations?'[8]   8. www.cpsi-fp7.eu/.

vu University Amsterdam is collaborating on the research project 'Converging and Conflicting Ethical Values in the Internal/External Security Continuum in Europe (INEX)'. Here, the thinking is not so much in terms of security-insecurity, but of a *security continuum*. Individuals are seen as mobile entities, as collections of data and characteristics, and ultimately as 'internal security issues'. According to the researchers: 'This security continuum has come about through the blurring of borders between external and internal security concerns, owing to the fact that external security authorities attempt to localize local threats at the level of internal security, while traditional internal security authorities have started to track down security threats externally.'[9]   9. www.inexproject.eu/.

The entire EU security programme costs European citizens €1.4 billion, a fraction of the money generated by the security industry. The results are not for citizens, the methodology is not public, the data mining algorithms – enabling end-users to extract usable information from large databases – are secret.

As of September 2009, new Dutch passports have RFID chips carrying the following information: name, passport number, nationality, date of birth, sex, expiration date, national citizen identification number, facial photo and fingerprints.[10] Only 32 per cent of today's Dutch citizens are worried about this.[11] Of their own accord, the police have broadened their task to include the creation of greater security: 'It's no small kettle of fish. Secretly checking up on everything and everybody, whenever and wherever. But according to police chiefs Bik, Kuijs and Welten, this is necessary in order to make the Netherlands even safer.'[12] A 2005 report on the development of the police and its functions speaks of 'identifying threats',[13] of wanting to operate in subordination to the proper authorities, of carrying out its tasks independently and accounting for its actions afterward.[14] Kuijs: 'We check everybody. That's the price you pay for the ability to identify a threat. People who have nothing to be afraid of are not inconvenienced at all. Citizens consider safety more important than privacy. I think they will get used to this system very quickly.' He also states: 'The predictive value of the information informs our actions.'[15] In a lecture on tracking and RFID, Prosecutor-General Harm Brouwer also speaks of proactive tracking, in which the accent shifts to predicting and preventing abnormal and threatening behavior.[16]

In this vision, the focus is no longer on people or identities, but on the trails that people leave behind them in going about their daily activities. Privacy is no longer a quality of an individual, but a continuum comprising a person, their things and their mobility. At the same time, we are seeing that identity is a changing composition of relations between a person, their things and an 'intelligent' environment. Both privacy and identity are continuums that are determined by multiple factors. An attempt to steer the environment would therefore

10. 'In addition, the chip contains a number of security-related files that can be used to determine whether it is an original chip and whether the data is unchanged. Although room is also reserved on the chip for address, telephone number, profession, custody/imprisonment, tax provisions and all sorts of other details, these fields, according to reports, will be left empty.'

11. Aukje van Roessel, 'Trek op die Muur! In Den Haag', 14 October 2009, www.groene.nl/2009/42/Trek-op-die-muur.

12. Weert Schenk, 'Veiligheid is belangrijker dan privacy', www.volkskrant.nl/archief_gratis/article1004800.ece/Veiligheid_is_belangrijker_dan_privacy 21 June 2005 and updated on 21 January 2005.

13. 'De Nederlandse politie beschermt leven, vrijheid en eigendom door te waken tegen kwaad.' In: *Politie in ontwikkeling. Visie op de politiefunctie*, Project group Visie op de politiefunctie, Raad van Hoofdcommissarissen (The Hague: NPI, May 2005).

14. 'Do the police want to break away from the power of the authorities? Welten: "Since the establishment of the regional police force in 1993, more has been done to develop the police profession than in the fifty years prior to that. We have taken this leeway for ourselves and we want to keep it in the future. The judiciary and the mayors remain the authorities. They stipulate what has to be done. But we want to determine how it is carried out. That's our profession. That's not a criticism of the administration.' The report makes no mention of what the main tasks of the police are. Welten: 'The spirit of the times determines what the main task of the police is. Main tasks can change by the day, so to speak. And that can be different in Amsterdam than it is in Drenthe. We want to do what is necessary for security.' Schenk, 'Veiligheid', op. cit. (note 12).

15. Ibid.

16. On 4 April 2007, the seminar 'RFID, Opsporing & Privacy' took place in Sociëteit de Witte in The Hague. The seminar was co-organized by ECP.NL and the RFID Platform Nederland. www.rathenau.nl/showpage.asp?item=2136.

seem inevitable. And that is what is happening now: public services, historical institutions like the police, states and supra-national states like the EU are trying to make a constant of the environment by building in security dashboards that are fed with data on the behaviour of citizens – who do not have access to these dashboards themselves. Citizens are contracting out their safety in the assumption that these dashboards will be effective. But this is not always the case. All of the data on Umar Farouk Abdulmutallab, the Nigerian who on Christmas day tried to carry out a terrorist attack above Detroit on Delta-Northwest flight 253, was present in the security dashboards, but without the intervention of one passenger, he would not have been stopped. Sometimes a system fails as a whole.

When a system only takes people's data trail seriously and no longer sees the people themselves, ultimately no one – including the administrators of the system – can believe in it anymore. This is nicely illustrated by the following: around the time that Genesee County treasurer Daniel Kildee was asked by the Obama administration to work out his plan for levelling 50 towns to the ground – simply because the government had given up on them – artist Jimini Hignett created the project *Special Attention*, in which she showed documentary images of an abandoned police station where the traces of identities – mug shots, fingerprints, witness testimonies – lie scattered among the dirt on the floor. All systems are vulnerable. Why should we believe that the central database in which the identities of the Dutch people are kept is secure? While the fear that the database will be 'cracked' has the upper hand right now, the possibility that the system that feeds it will crack is much more real.

Bringing Policy in Line with Reality

Is there an alternative? Here is my proposal: make the data, methodologies and algorithms that are acquired with public money totally open to the public. This can lead to the creation of new social services. A brainstorm session with professionals showed that there are real chances for a good use of connectivity pushed through to the district level – for example, collectively coordinating chores like grocery shopping, taking kids to school, and sharing and loaning out all sorts of equipment.[17] Another kind of service could consist of offering real-time threat analyses, showing that the threat of a terrorist attack for individuals is 0.0001 per cent and slipping and falling in the bathroom is 0.3 per cent. At an airport where

17. Rob van Kranenburg, *Het Internet der Dingen, wat is het? Een dag uit het leven van een gezin in het Internet der Dingen*, www.waag.org/download/63929.

Jimini Hignett, *Special Attention.*

people use Layar, Twitter and Linkedin – and where nobody wants to be blown up – the worst thing that can happen is that erroneous information about fellow passengers is obtained from the accessible databases. In such an environment, more and more fatal misunderstandings can occur. Umar Farouk Abdulmutallab slipped through the net of the regular security dashboards. If we were to once again feel responsible for our own actions and safety, perhaps we would have intercepted him earlier.

As ordinary citizens, we in principle have the possibility to make combinations of open source software, network algorithms and hardware.[18] In the code, which we ourselves could administer down to the lowest level, lie possibilities of building in forms of solidarity and making them part of applications and services. For why couldn't we also code social variables into the dominant protocols? With the Internet of Things, the big challenge for designers, thinkers and makers is to play a part at the lowest level, to determine what the protocols will look like, what kind of wireless frequencies go to users, and what kind of data goes from users to the database. Specifically for this purpose, I have set up the Council think-tank: 'We believe the "winning solution" to making the most open, inclusive and innovative Internet of Things is to transcend the short-term opposition between social innovation and security by finding a way to combine these two necessities in a broader common perspective.'[19]

This new perspective ultimately can be nothing other than a guideline for bringing policy in line with reality. In addition to constants that have functioned well in every age, such as delaying, arbitrating, negotiating and finding a balance between short and long term, it is particularly important to allow for conflicts, just like in any other frontier community. Robert Dykstra writes in *The Cattle Towns*: 'Social conflict was normal, it was inevitable, and it was a format for community decision making.'[20] The sociologist Lewis Coser advises: 'Instead of viewing

18. If we combine the dyne:bolic OS, the RFID Guardian and the Bricophone, we get a completely open generic telephone to which we can connect all sorts of functionalities and make free telephone calls. Why pay when the air is free? The dyne:bolic operating system is an easy-to-install GNU/Linux system that works even on the oldest of computers. The RFID Guardian by Melanie Rieback (VU) is an open source hardware RFID hacking toolkit that can also be used as a lifestyle manager. You decide which RFID tags you want to accept and which you do not. The Bricophone is an open source, mesh-networking infrastructure for mobile telephony, especially for smaller communities, based on the principal that every node in the network simultaneously sends and receives. http://code.dyne.org/; http://www.rfidguardian.org/index.php/Main_Page; http://www.nlnet.nl/project/bricophone/.

19. http://www.theinternetofthings.eu/what-we-want.

20. In: Don Harrison Doyle, *The Social Order of a Frontier Community: Jacksonville, Illinois, 1825-70*, (Champaign, IL: University of Illinois Press, 1983), 11.21. Ibid. 'When Jacksonville's Colonel W.B. Warren publicly horsewhipped and caned a newspaper editor who had dishonored his family's name, he clearly perceived and expressed conflict in highly personalized terms. In contrast, the propensity to organize conflict through vigilance societies, political parties or voluntary associations signified a more sophisticated form of conflict that integrated local society as it defined social boundaries.'

conflict as a disruptive event signifying disorganization, we should appreciate it as a positive process by which members of the community ally with one another, identify common values and interests, and organize to contest power with competing groups.'[21]

A new division of roles between citizens, states, democratic institutions and industry is forcing itself upon us. This will not happen without conflicts. And citizens, in their turn, must learn how to deal with a distributed form of what is one's own, and get used to the fact that their privacy is changing into privacies.

21. Ibid. 'When Jacksonville's Colonel W.B. Warren publicly horsewhipped and caned a newspaper editor who had dishonored his family's name, he clearly perceived and expressed conflict in highly personalized terms. In contrast, the propensity to organize conflict through vigilance societies, political parties or voluntary associations signified a more sophisticated form of conflict that integrated local society as it defined social boundaries.'

book reviews

Wouter Davidts and Kim Paice (eds.)
The Fall of the Studio: Artists at Work

Dominic van den Boogerd

(Amsterdam: Valiz, 2009).
ISBN: 978-90-78088-29-5,
250 pages, € 17.50

Since the advent of performance, conceptual art, land art and minimal art in the 1960s, the studio has been put in a bad light. The traditional workplace was seen as old-fashioned and limiting for the development of new forms of art. Painting and sculpture, the time-honoured studio disciplines, were declared passé, along with the corresponding tools and techniques. Robert Smithson declared in 1968 that deliverance from the confines of the studio freed the artist 'from the snares of craft and the bondage of creativity'. Daniel Buren concluded in his controversial essay 'Fonction de l'atelier' (1971) that working on location amounted to the 'destruction' of the studio. The studio was declared dead, the post-studio practice was born.

Just who introduced the term 'post-studio' is uncertain. John Baldessari maintains it was Carl Andre, but that is not plausible. Buren and Smithson, who wrote a good deal about the matter, never used the term themselves. What can be said with certainty is that the criticism of the studio was related to the desired transformation of art: handwork was to become mental exercise, while

the making of the art work would simply be outsourced. Of all the institutes of the art world that were critically examined in those years, only the studio acquired the prefix 'post'. There is no such thing as 'post-museum', unless one might be speaking of a collection of old postage stamps.

The essays in this book examine the shifts in the nature and use of the artist's studio over the past half of a century, concentrating on individual artists from Robert Morris to Jan de Cock. Although the book does not delve deeply into Smithson, who after all was one of the instigators of the post-studio practice, it gives an intriguing picture of a changing studio practice as a symptom of radical developments in (and outside) art. A few authors report from first-hand experience – Philip Ursprung, for example, visited Olafur Eliasson in his studio – but the vast majority of the writers analyse the workspace by means of studio photos, artists' texts or works of art. And what do we find? Artists who are identified with the old mores, like Mark Rothko, turn out to have maintained a much more complex studio practice,

while post-studio celebrities like Buren have not at all taken such a great distance from the studio as often is thought.

Rothko might be considered emblematic for the artist's romantic isolation and existential struggle, culminating in his suicide in his studio. Morgan Thomas, however, convincingly argues that Rothko's paintings do not so much reflect the introspection of the artist and the isolation of the studio, but the complex exchange between the place where the painting was made and the place for which it was created. While working on a commission for a chapel in Houston that still needed to be constructed, Rothko had the walls of the chapel erected in his studio, a dusky former gym in the Bowery in New York. The space was fitted out accordingly, with rope and tackle systems, movable walls and rolling floor lamps. Rothko's painter's studio was like a film studio, set up to achieve specific pictorial effects, and in a careful analysis of those painterly qualities, Thomas boldly makes comparisons with Alfred Hitchcock's way of working. It is one of the most stimulating essays in the book.

According to Buren, a work

of art is doomed to be in places where it does not belong, manipulated by people to whom it does not belong, forever estranged from its origin, the studio. Buren tried to maintain control by working *in situ*, but, as Wouter Davidts argues, he still was not saying farewell to everything the traditional studio stands for – namely, the authority and genius of the individual author. The bond between the art work and the studio was simply replaced by the bond between the art work and the artist. The artist, no longer working like a monk in his cell, became a travelling, networking interventionist. 'My studio is in fact wherever I am,' said Buren. All that his emblematic motif says is: *Buren was here.* The more intensely he denounces the studio, the more clear it becomes how much his work is determined by it.

The contributions become more speculative as the present draws closer. Julia Gelshorn discusses a number of artworks from the 1990s that have the 'masculine mystique' of the studio as their theme. While such heroism might resonate in Matthew Barney's studio cum gymnasium, where the artist clambers over the ceiling like a trained alpinist, it is also clear that in itself this metaphor for artistic effort is rather forced. Kippenberger would seem to underscore this in *Spiderman Studio* (1996), in which the artist is depicted as the eponymous superhero in an attic studio. The installation was first shown in a building in Nice where Henri Matisse once had his studio, under the title *L'atelier Matisse sous-loué à Spiderman*. According to the inscriptions on the paintings surrounding the artist/superhero, his special powers have a rather trivial origin: red wine, sleeping pills, hash and other intoxication-inducing products for which Kippenberger had a penchant. The artist gifted with exceptional talent, personified by Matisse, is replaced here by the artist poisoned by addictive substances, an ordinary mortal who can only pretend to be extraordinary, like the nerd who transmutes into Spiderman. Or, as Kippenberger's reversal of Beuys's famous slogan goes: *Jeder Künstler ist ein Mensch.*

What this well-edited book makes clear is that the post-studio practice should not be taken all too literally, but as an indication of changing views about art and artistry. For no matter how much the workspace of art may have shifted, every artist still has an address. All of the artists discussed in this book had or have a workplace of their own that combines various functions (Eliasson, an employer of architects and art historians, calls his studio a 'centre for knowledge production'). Corporate concourses, offices and other written-off branches of trade and industry are the cuckoo's nests of today's art. Cities where there is plenty of 'cheap' space for rent, like Berlin, Glasgow and Detroit, are the art centres of the future. Even a radical conceptual like Stanley Brouwn rents a workspace of his own. In order to think outside the box of the studio, you need a studio.

Pascal Gielen
The Murmuring of the Artistic Multitude: Global Art, Memory and Post-Fordism

(Amsterdam: Valiz, 2009).
ISBN 978-90-78088-34-9,
368 pages, € 19,90

Pascal Gielen and Paul de Bruyne (eds.)
Arts in Society: Being an Artist in Post-Fordist Times

(Rotterdam: NAi Publishers, 2009).
ISBN 978-90-5662-71109,
208 pages, € 23,50

Merijn Oudenampsen

In the European cultural field at the end of the 1990s, two new phenomena were to make their stage appearance. On the one hand, the creative industries approach was developed, first in London through the infamous white papers of the Department of Culture Media and Sports (DCMS) under New Labour, and not much later through the work of Richard Florida. It was a response to the increasingly central role of cultural production in the economy, a development neatly synthesized by Amsterdam's *überplanner* Zef Hemel: 'The economy is becoming increasingly cultural, and culture is becoming increasingly commercial.' With the creative industries policy, a new entrepreneurial approach to culture and the arts was born, which would set out to conquer large parts of Europe's cultural policy apparatus. Artists and cultural workers themselves, now described as 'cultural entrepreneurs' or 'creative class', were proclaimed as role models of the new economy. They were said to embody the new work ethic, based on flexibility, entrepreneurialism, networking, the ability to deal with uncertainty, lifelong learning, creativity, innovation and so on.

On the other hand, there was the resurgence and international popularization of radical theory. One current gained particular prominence, epitomized by the success of the book *Empire* by Antonio Negri and Michael Hardt. This current is known under many names, some call it post-operaist, others post-autonomia, others sympathetically label it 'heretical Marxism'. In many ways, this school of thought anticipated and theorized the abovementioned economic transformations and that of labour subjectivity more broadly. Through a series of conferences – such as DASH, NEURO, DOCUMENTA XI – post-operaismo became the lingua franca of a politically engaged subscene in the European art world. The presence in 2009 of some of the main post-operaist stars at Tate Britain – Maurizio Lazzarato, Judith Revel, Franco 'Bifo' Beradi and Antonio Negri – to discuss the relation between art and labour, is evidence of its still growing popularity today.

In the Netherlands, the first development has come to define the new standard in the cultural sector. Planners and policymakers, and even artists themselves have largely adopt-ed the entrepreneurial mindset as proposed by Florida and New Labour. The second phenomenon, however, has never caught on, leaving us with little analytical tools to come to a critical understanding of the transformation that has taken place. This challenge has now been taken up by art sociologist Pascal Gielen, who in two recent books, *The Murmuring of the Artistic Multitude*, and *Being an Artist in Post-Fordist Times* (edited with Pascal de Bruyne), has made an attempt at introducing some of the post-operaist lexicon to the Dutch art world.

The central subject Gielen elaborates on in his books, is that of post-Fordism. The concept basically describes the new flexible economy that has supplanted the old industrial mode of production – Fordism, a term coined by Antonio Gramsci and named after the factories of carmaker Henry Ford. Under Fordism, there was the figure of the mass worker, appointed with a pretty brainless and repetitive task – think of Charlie Chaplin's *Modern Times*. Under post-Fordism, the creative and communicative skills of the worker have become much more important to coordinate an ever more complex, decentralized and dynamic production process. It is nicely summarized in a quip by the Italian philosopher Paolo Virno, who refers to the signs hanging on the walls of the factories of old: 'Silence, work in progress'. In the new spaces of production, he suggests, it should read 'Work in progress. Speak'.

The essay compilation *The Murmuring of the Artistic Multitude* covers a series of topics, starting out with post-Fordism, passing through memory and heritage, towards the globalization of art and the biennials. Gielen introduces some of the basic Italian post-operaist concepts, (relying mostly on the work of Virno and staying well clear of Negri's more messianic approach): post-Fordism, Multitude, Biopolitics, Virtuosity, Opportunism. In the memory and heritage section, he uses the work of Goffman to analyse the relation between art and memory, giving mostly Flemish examples. And lastly, focusing on the biennales, Gielen relates some interesting interviews with key Belgian curators, Jan Hoet and Barbara Vanderlinden, and develops a scheme to interpret the new rules of the globalized art system, relating it back to the art-sociology of Heinich and Bourdieu.

The edited volume *Being an Artist in Post Fordist Times*, is a combination of essays by different authors (Michael Hardt, Rudi Laermans and Paul de Bruyne) – and interviews with leading contemporary artists such as Michelangelo Pistoletto, Anne Teresa de Keersmaeker, Pippo Delbono, Matthew Herbert, Thierry de Cordier, Sang Jia en Pun Siu Fai. However, the setup with the essays and the interviews does not seem to work very well for the editors, with most of the artists having their own phlegmatic and eclectic positions, bearing little relation if any, with the post-Fordist *zeitgeist* Gielen and de Bruyne are trying to discuss (though granted, Gielen does refer to the post-Fordist embrace of idiosyncrasy). In comparison with the well-crafted *The Murmuring*, this book is decidedly more unbalanced.

Echoing the work of French sociologist Luc Boltanksi, Pascal Gielen's central thesis is that the art world has acted as a sort of behavioural laboratory where the creative behaviour that is now standard requirement in post-Fordist capitalism was first developed. The central role of art and culture in the new economy has therefore been long coming, suggests Gielen. He cites Virno, stating that 'art has been diluted in society like a soluble tablet in a glass of water'. Accordingly, Gielen's mission is to find out what to do with this newfound economic and cultural centrality of the arts. What is to be done with a soluble tablet? Having seen the art practice change from a rather marginal affair to that of semi-professional practice, and he himself residing over an impressive growth of art students as lecturer on Art and Society at the Fontys art school in Tilburg, Gielen tries to map out the consequences of the professionalization of the arts for artistic autonomy and practice. It's a spirited search for cracks, tears and holes, in which a critically engaged art practice can survive and thrive.

Finally, as Gielen explains, murmuring is a extralinguistic vitalistic buzz, a form of resistance, a way of being that can makes itself heard while escaping recuperation and cooptation. Let's hope this multitudinous buzz keeps on buzzing, distributing itself along the fault lines in the arts system and society at large. Let's spread the buzz.

Brian Holmes
Escape the Overcode: Activist Art in the Control Society

Willem van Weelden

(Paris, Eindhoven, Zagreb, Istanbul: Van Abbemuseum Public Research # 2 / What, How & for Whom / WHW, 2009).
ISBN: 978-90-70149-98-7, 416 pages, € 15

This new collection of essays by cultural critic and activist Brian Holmes was published by the Van Abbemuseum in collaboration with the Zagreb-based curators' collective What, How and for Whom (WHW) as the second publication in the Van Abbemuseum Public Research Series (VAMPR). The series focuses on bringing new knowledge about the political possibilities of art and its institutes into the public domain. *Escape the Overcode* is appearing at a time when there is renewed interest in the work of Gilles Deleuze and Félix Guattari. Particularly Guattari (1930-1992), unpublished work of whose was recently made available, is an urgent reference for Holmes in his analysis of the present-day production of subjectivity and of its de-programming. The 21 essays in *Escape the Overcode* first appeared on his blog *Continental Drift*, and were composed over a period of two years. The collection is a 'quod erat demonstrandum' of a Guattarian analysis of contemporary world capitalism.

In those two years, Holmes travelled a great deal (Europe, the USA, Asia, Latin America), conducting extensive 'extradisciplinary' research into various activist art practices on the spot. Using this as a basis, he has made a diagnostic portrait of the times that provides insight into the possibilities for a truly effective, subversive art: art that is a counterforce to the 'overcoding' produced by today's global capitalism. The term 'overcoding' is a fairly problematic concept borrowed by Holmes from the work of Deleuze and Guattari – in particular, the essay 'Apparatus of Capture' in *Mille Plateaux*. Its problematic aspect lies in its ambiguity: on the one hand, it refers, in line with Deleuze and Guattari, to the threat posed by the totalitarian forcing into line and standardization brought about by a completely integrated world capitalism through the overwriting of all domains with a single code. On the other hand, it can be used to designate the overwriting that occurs when dominant codes of institutional regimes of meaning mix with local meanings. Holmes primarily deals with the former, which he sees confirmed in Guattari's later work – in which Guattari talks about the last phase in the development of capitalism, when overcoding reaches a maximum.

This totalitarian overcoding, also described as cognitive capitalism, not only plays a role at the scale of economic transactions but also at the scale of the production of a specific, controlled form of subjectivization, of an experiential regime. The overcoding is a unifying movement that makes marginal voices and experiences subordinate to a single overcode, a kind of supercode that not only has repercussions for symbolic communication, but also for the ways in which imperative models of interaction regulate, standardize and organize. An important component of this theory is that our network society, with its ubiquitous computer communication and symbolic exchange, lends itself extremely well to complete control over specific forms of subjectivization. In his essays, Holmes reports on artistic practices that operate in the border zones of what still can be termed art, but that all support or effect a transformative process that disrupts the 'overcoding' and shirks institutional control. An art that in many cases shuns the white walls of the museum, and in its appearance in public space relates to its viewers in a different way. These are practices that can be interpreted as reprogrammings of the imperative subjectivity propagated by the global information machine. For Holmes, this reprogramming is particularly aimed at a sensory, affective recalibration.

Escape the Overcode starts off with three introductions, each of which deals with one part of the book's underlying theoretical framework. The first forms the basis for Holmes's interpretation of art practices that appear to escape the overcode; in the second he presents a case in point, Marcelo Expósito's film *First of May* (also published in *Open* no. 17); lastly follows a more traditional introduction in which he affords the reader insight into his argumentation. The first introduction is also an affective manifesto, in which Holmes breaks a lance for a new concept of art based on the thesis that expression is an affective gesture that has the inherent quality of freeing contacts between people. In short, artistic activism is *affectivism*, and as such opens new, expanding territories of alternative views and experience. In this seemingly simple equating of terms, Holmes relies heavily on the preliminary work Guattari developed in his alternative psychiatric clinic La Borde and his activist practices (free radio, eco-activism, schizo-analytic cartography). In that work, Guattari describes the importance and significance of art in our times: in his view, art offers the only workable model for throwing off a prevailing subjectivity, by offering new modalities of experience that are based on an autonomous practice and rooted in the here and now.

For Holmes, the functioning of locally bound cultural practices and their liberating effect are directly related to a global front where the reprogramming of the symbolic order needs to be fought out. For despite his decidedly engaged political agenda, Holmes apparently considers regular politics no longer capable of being a significant factor for any form of positive social emancipation or change. Like an anthropologist of Guattari's 'integrated world capitalism', Holmes has composed a book that attempts to weave together a cartography of subversive global art practices by means of local examples. In order to give shape to this theoretical cross-linking, Holmes shuttles – sometimes a little too didactically, sometimes uneasily or almost ecstatically – between different and hard-to-compare scales of aggregation. He himself calls it 'an almost fractal interplay of scales'.

The reader must therefore be prepared for the fact that *Escape the Overcode* can jump from a molecular, affective scale to a more surveying, cartographic scale of interpretation and analysis (in this regard, Holmes introduces the neologism 'geocritique'). Like Guattari, he jumps from psychoanalytic theories to theoretical system analyses, then links up factoids from popular economics with biological models. This extradisciplinary approach seems to tie in with how the art world currently speaks of 'artistic research', which to hard-core scientists often is an abomination of superficial appropriations and half-understood applications. Holmes's form of discussion avoids such scientific assessments precisely because it attempts to be an expression of an aesthetic/ethical imperative aimed at attacking sacred cows, with the goal of fuelling a new sensibility and passion for investigation out of a deep sense of urgency. The book is not so much an exegesis of a 'grand theory' about the production of subjectivity under new geopolitical conditions, as it is a personal account of an inspired phase in a researcher's practice. *Escape the Overcode* above all is a call for experiments of thought and offers a variegated toolbox for conducting them. In the wake of the revival and reintroduction of the mental legacy of Deleuze and Guattari, there is a good chance that Holmes's toolbox will be an inspiring aid for many people in lending significance to the molecular revolutions in the arts.

Marie-Christine Bureau, Marc Perrenoud and Roberta Shapiro (eds.)
L'artiste pluriel. Démultiplier l'activité pour vivre de son art

Pascal Gielen

(Villeneuve d'Ascq: Presses Universitaires du Septentrion, 2009).
ISBN: 978-2-7574-0086-9, 194 pages, € 19,-

It is a well-known fact that the working life of the artist is many-sided. Actors, painters or dancers have always been jobbing in the catering industry or education to help them achieve their real dream: to be an autonomous artist. In economic terms this would mean the artist can live off his or her art. In *L'artiste pluriel: Démultiplier l'activité pour vivre de son art* (The Plural Artist: Diversifying Your Vocation to Make Art Your Living) a number of researchers demonstrate that this plural professional practice applies to almost all disciplines in the world of art. Musicians, comedians, artists, actors, architects and dancers – whether classical or hip hop – all come under scrutiny. And in all these different professional fields the researchers find plural activities. Differentiated professional practice is what lies at the core of artistic existence. But how do we define 'plural'? Marie-Christine Bureau and Roberta Shapiro comment in the book that different notions of this concept can exist side by side. In their introductory chapter they aim to create conceptual clarity by pointing to the distinction that needs to be made between polyvalence, polyactivity and pluriactivity. Artists employed in a *polyvalent* capacity carry out different tasks within their own artistic discipline. One could, for example,

be an actor and also do administrative work at the same theatre company. The *polyactive* artist, on the other hand, fills a number of posts in different fields. The well-known example of the artist who also waits tables in a restaurant comes under this category. And the term *pluriactivity,* finally, is reserved by the authors to distinguish between activities within their own artistic 'metier', such as the musician who is also a sound engineer.

Interestingly, Bureau and Shapiro point out that pluriactivity has an economic as well as a legal or even political dimension (though they do not literally use these words). Thus economic motives underlie pluriactivity: in short, one keeps down several jobs in order to make a living. In addition, the legal or social status of an artist plays a role. In those countries or regimes where the government guarantees job security, pluriactivity is less prevalent. It is not surprising that in Russia, for example, pluriactivity doubled between 1992 and 1996. So the redefinition of the artistic profession that has taken place during the last few years has something to do with the extent to which government intervention has changed. A political shift has come about, but this factor is barely examined by the different authors

in *L'artiste pluriel.* The authors identify a third dimension over and above the economic and political. If an increasing pluriactivity fuels the debate over the identity and autonomy of the artist, then the status of the artist in society becomes unclear. This, then, could be characterized as a sociocultural dimension.

Although Bureau and Shapiro establish some conceptual clarity by differentiating within the artistic profession, the various authors in the book each tackle the subject in their own way. And this causes, to put it mildly, considerable disparity in their approaches and points of departure – in terms of both methodology and research focus. Thus Janine Rannou and Ionela Roharik approach the phenomenon in the world of dance from a largely quantitative angle, while Emmanuel Sulzer makes use of in-depth interviews. And while the latter chooses to focus on the art academy, others address issues relating to employment or policy contexts. This heterogeneity turns *L'artiste pluriel* into a somewhat . . . plural book. The majority of the individual contributions do furnish interesting insights into the specific art worlds they study, but the great diversity in approach excludes the possibility of a comparative framework. Questions such as: is professional practice in the theatre world more or less pluriactive than that in, let's say, the world of fine arts – remain unanswered. In spite of much sound and empirically well-supported data, the book does not rise above being a loosely connected assortment of impressions concerning artistic professional practices within divergent disciplines. This 'impressionistic' approach, moreover, is strengthened because most of the articles fail to include a historical dimension. That professional practice today is pluriactive is demonstrated with great zeal, but very little empirical evidence is offered for answering the question of whether it is more so now than in the past. Neither is it clear, therefore, whether a growing pluriactivity is taking place in response to society today, or whether that activity is suddenly being extensively recorded because it has become a cause of interest to sociologists and other academics. The question is: Are we faced here with a self-fulfilling prophecy? In other words, are sociologists finding more plu-

riactivity today because we are looking for it?

Furthermore, we do not find out in *L'artiste pluriel* whether the contents of pluriactivity have changed over time. Were artists in the past, for example, employed chiefly in the catering and education sectors, and are they today maybe increasingly sought after by the creative industry? In other words, are artists today being absorbed in the mainstream economy on the strength of their specific artistic, creative capabilities? Antonella Corsan and Marizio Lazzarato do touch on the influence of the cultural industry on professional practice in the margins of their description of the current problematic phenomenon of project work and contracts. But even they do not reach beyond a neat typology of the so-called 'intermittents'. In other words, a macro-sociological and macro-economic perspective is lacking in the book. This is a shortcoming of more than one of the contributions in *L'artiste pluriel*, which is why the book barely gets beyond the descriptive level. Apart

from the occasional reference to a retreating government, the reader is presented with little in the way of explanatory factors for the present-day work situation of the artist. And this while there are several lines of interpretation, theoretical pistes even, for the taking. Thus we have labour-sociological and also philosophical theories on post-Fordian labour conditions, as well as social and politic-oeconomic phenomena such as globalization and worldwide neoliberalization, which could offer a more consistent interpretative framework for the pluriactivity they identify. Angles like these could have added to the coherence between the widely divergent pieces in *L'artiste pluriel*. This is not to say that the book does not provide us with interesting insights into the current – sometimes precarious – professional situation of the artist today. The greatest merit of *L'artiste pluriel* may well lie in the fact that it tickles the appetite for further research about the doings of that curious profession that is the artist's in society today.

Konrad Becker and Felix Stalder (eds.)
Deep Search: The Politics of Search Beyond Google

Willem van Weelden

(Innsbruck/Vienna/Munich: Studienverlag & Transaction Publishers, 2009)
ISBN 978-3-7065-4795-6, 220 pages, € 24.90

In November of 2009, the important conference 'Search of the Query', organized by the Institute of Network Cultures, took place in Amsterdam, where Konrad Becker, cofounder of the World Information Institute in Vienna, presented *Deep Search: The Politics of Search Beyond Google*, a collection of essays compiled by Felix Stalder and himself, which had just rolled off the press. This book, the result of a similarly named conference previously held in Vienna, is divided into four sections, 'Histories', 'Liberties', 'Power' and 'Visibility', that go deeper into various aspects of the ubiquitous and monumental presence of search engines.

We have all become accustomed in our daily lives to using Google, which

holds a unique position as the most frequently used search machine on the Internet. Neither the economic crisis nor the company's clashes with the leaders of China changes a thing about this. The search machine has become an indispensable social phenomenon in a global information society where cost-cutting nation-states are no longer so willing or able to bear the responsibility of providing free information for their subjects. Paying for education as well as managing libraries and heritage and keeping them up to date has become an almost prohibitively expensive job,

partly because of the enormous quantitative expansion of available information. But we must also bend our minds to the complex and sweeping transformation of a linear, centrally organized book culture into a strictly horizontal, widely distributed digital culture.

People often sigh that free access to information and knowledge has become problematic due to the intervention and monopoly of commercial companies like Google. In the politics of the search command, is there still an alternative beyond the services that Google ostensibly offers for 'free'? Google is expanding its services almost by the week, such as its recent project to make millions of books freely available online. Not only is the business monopoly position of the Google success story cause for concern, but also the fact that it has become so dominant that it is hardly possible to think of the generic, intellectual or private use of the Google search machine and the company's specific business practices as a conceptual totality anymore. In this connection, we must look to the long awaited book by Siva Vaidhyanathan, *The Googlization of Everything*, which is coming out shortly. Unfortunately, the author is not represented in the *Deep Search* compilation, but he did give a presentation on this interesting project at the

'Search of the Query' conference. His anticipation of the Googlization of our lives arises from the worrying conclusion that the searching for and finding of information, as well as issues concerning the cultural and political aspects of the classification of information, deserves a much more fundamental and deeper discussion than the business model of a single company, which in all of its actions simply strives to maximize profits and therefore does everything in its power to be able to 'read' the end-user who is typing in the search command.

In various critical essays by, among others, Geert Lovink, Lev Manovich, Richard Rogers, Metahaven, Matteo Pasquinelli, Konrad Becker and Felix Stalder/Christine Mayer, *Deep Search* not only draws attention to these and other problems concerning the supplying and finding of information. The book also focuses on long-term issues and the political ramifications they bring with them. For in the arena of search commands and search machines, the rapidity with which technologies, distribution forms and user forms are changing is merely a signal that the development of the technological information complex is by no means finished. One can even question whether the transformational state in which the Internet, as the new standard of our information supply, has found itself for more than a decade is not an inherent condition of its architecture. Since time immemorial, technological developments have laid the groundwork in the search for, storage and organizing of knowledge and information. Thus, it is only logical that we also examine both the past's analogue and the present's digital manner of looking up information from an evolutionary perspective.

Deep Search accordingly focuses on both the technological dimensions of this change in our information supply and the social and cultural aspects that underlie the construction of information and knowledge. All of the essays in the book share the fundamental insight that the context, culture and classification of information systems are determining factors for how individuals and collectives discover and experience the world. As a 'mass medium' and as a relatively new technology in the network society, the search machine is gaining an increasingly critical and defining role whereby its effect on politics and the economy will surpass that of the conventional news sector and of the old mass media.

Geert Lovink, media theorist and director of the Institute of Network Cultures, refers to MIT professor and computer critic Joseph Weizenbaum (1923-2008) in his essay. Weizenbaum was not only a prophetic computer academic, but also an early critic of the limitations of artificial intelligence, who even argued for a separate ethics for that field. Lovink cites Weizenbaum in order to examine critically the difference between 'deciding' and 'choosing' in the light of the logic of the search machine. Computers cannot choose; this is a process that can only be a human affair because it requires moral awareness and judgment. A simple notion perhaps, but a valuable qualification of the far-reaching computerization and mechanization of society.

Deep Search marks an important *Wende* in Internet criticism, and can be considered a pioneering contribution to a research terrain that, parallel to a further politicization of our dealings with technology, will only increase in importance in the coming years.

PERSONALIA

Dominic van den Boogerd is the director of the post-academic artists' institute De Ateliers in Amsterdam. He writes regularly for art magazines such as *Metropolis M*, *Art Papers* and *Stedelijk Museum Bulletin*. His essays have appeared in the exhibition catalogues of Michael Raedecker, Fiona Tan, Manfred Pernice, Marlene Dumas, Keith Tyson, Matthew Day Jackson and others.

Matthijs Bouw is director of One Architecture. He works on a wide variety of architectural and urban design assignments, ranging from transforming a national monument to investigating new key projects for the Ministry of Housing, Spatial Development and the Environment (VROM). One Architecture is working on the City Development Strategy for Tbilisi.

Pascal Gielen is affiliated with the University of Groningen (RUG) as an art sociologist and is director of the research group 'Arts in Society' at the Fontys University of Applied Sciences in Tilburg. His last two publications are *The Murmuring of the Artistic Multitude: Global Art, Memory and Post-Fordism* (2009) and *Arts in Society: Being an Artist in Post-Fordist Times* (2009, co-edited with Paul De Bruyne). See the review in this issue.

Joris van Hoboken is a PhD candidate at the Institute for information Law (IViR). His research focuses on search engine regulation and freedom of expression. He is specifically interested in issues relating to Internet media and fundamental rights. Joris is also a member of the board at Bits of Freedom.

Rob van Kranenburg lives in Ghent. He is part of Timelab.org. As project director of the EU PEOPLE project SHARE IT, he works in the research group Ambient Intelligence led by Ben Schouten. In collaboration with friends, he founded brico-labs.net and Council (www.theinternetofthings.eu). He can be reached at kranenbu@xs4all.nl

Rudi Laermans is a full professor of sociological theory at the Faculty of Social Sciences at Katholieke Universiteit Leuven. His research and publications are primarily situated within the domains of contemporary social and cultural theory and the sociology of art.

Maurizio Lazzarato is a sociologist and member of the editorial staff of the magazine *Multitudes*. He lives and works in Paris. 1996 saw the publication of his famous essay 'Immaterial Labour', whose theme he further developed in *Lavoro Immateriale. Forme di vita e produzione di soggettività* (Verona), which appeared a year later.

Oliver Leistert studied philosophy, computer science and German literature. He was a research fellow at the Central European University in Budapest and at Sarai, an institute for new media and urbanity in Delhi. As a member of the DFG Graduiertenkolleg 'Automatismen' at University Paderborn, he researches the mobile media practice of social movements and its surveillance. For this research he conducted a series of interviews in cities around the globe.

Armin Medosch is a researcher in digital arts and network culture, based in London and Vienna. His latest projects include the exhibition 'Waves' and the collaborative research platform 'Thenextlayer': www.thenextlayer.org/.

Merijn Oudenampsen is a freelance researcher who focuses on populism and urban development. Until 2009 he was affiliated with the Jan van Eyck Academy in Maastricht, where he researched populism within the framework of the project 'Design Negation'. Currently he is working on a book about populism and the politics of symbols. His writings can be found online and offline in *de Groene Amsterdammer*, *Metropolis M*, *Denktank Waterland*, *Archined* and *Mute Magazine*.

Mark Shepard is an artist, architect and researcher whose work explores the implications of mobile media and embedded information systems for architecture and urbanism. He is an assistant professor of architecture and media study at the State University of New York in Buffalo.

Daniel J. Solove is a professor of law at George Washington University Law School. In 2008 he published *Understanding Privacy*; see: understanding-privacy.com. Solove is also the author of *The Future of Reputation: Gossip, Rumor and Privacy on the Internet* (2007).

Felix Stalder lives in Vienna and is a lecturer in theories of media and society at the Zurich University of the Arts. He is a researcher and activist focusing on new forms of cultural production, surveillance, control and subjectivity, and new patterns of spatial organization. He has been a moderator of the nettime mailing list since 1998 and has organized numerous international conferences in Europe and beyond. See felix.openflows.com for publications.

Martijn de Waal is a writer and researcher. He is part of the New Media, Public Sphere and Urban Culture research project in the Department of Practical Philosophy at the University of Groningen. He is cofounder of TheMobileCity.nl – an international think-tank for new media and urban culture. (www.martijndewaal.nl)

Willem van Weelden is an artist, researcher and writer.

CREDITS

Open Cahier on Art and the Public
Domain
Volume 9 (2010) no. 19

Editors Jorinde Seijdel (editor
in chief), Liesbeth Melis (final
editing)
With thanks to Geert Lovink for
his valuable advice and Merijn
Oudenampsen for editing the essays
by Oliver Leistert and Maurizio
Lazzarato.

English copy editor D'Laine Camp

Dutch-English translations Jane
Bemont (editorial, texts by Rudi
Laermans, Martijn de Waal and Rob
van Kranenburg, column by Joris van
Hoboken, book reviews by Dominic
van den Boogerd and by Willem van
Weelden); Karen Maters (book review
by Pascal Gielen)
French-English translation Walter
van der Star (text Maurizio
Lazzarato)

Graphic design Thomas Buxó and
Klaartje van Eijk

Printing and lithography Die Keure,
Brugge

Project coordinator Marieke van
Giersbergen, NAi Publishers

Publisher Eelco van Welie, NAi
Publishers

Open is published twice a year
Open 20 will be published in
November 2010

Editorial address
SKOR
Ruysdaelkade 2
1072 AG Amsterdam
the Netherlands
Tel +31 (0)20 6722525
Fax +31 (0)20 3792809
open@skor.nl / www.opencahier.nl

SUBSCRIPTIONS

Abonnementenland
Postbus 20
1910 AA Uitgeest
the Netherlands
0900-2265263 – € 0,10 per minute)
Fax +31 (0)251 310405
www.aboland.nl.

PRICE PER ISSUE
€ 23.50

SUBSCRIPTION PRICES
(postage included)
the Netherlands: € 32.50
Within Europe: € 39.50
Outside Europe: € 45.00
Students: € 24.50

SUBSCRIPTION CANCELLATION

Cancellations (in writing only) must
be received by Abonnementenland
eight weeks prior to the end of the
subscription period. Subscriptions
not cancelled in time are automatically renewed for one year.

For a comprehensive overview
of contents according to
author, article and theme,
see www.opencahier.nl

open

(IN)SECURITY

(NO) MEMORY

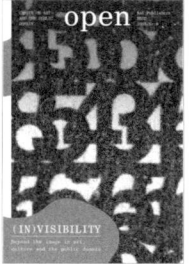

(IN)VISIBILITY

SOUND

(IN)TOLERANCE

HYBRID SPACE

FREEDOM
OF CULTURE

THE RISE OF THE
INFORMAL MEDIA

ART AS
A PUBLIC ISSUE

SOCIAL
ENGINEERING

THE ART BIENNIAL
AS GLOBAL
PHENOMENON

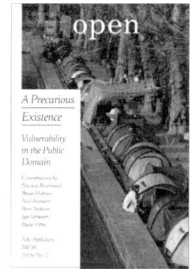

A PRECARIOUS
EXISTENCE

2030: WAR ZONE

NAi Publishers is an internationally orientated
publisher specialized in developing, producing and
distributing books on architecture, visual arts and
related disciplines.
www.naipublishers.nl info@naipublishers.nl

It was not possible to find all the copyright holders of the illustrations used. Interested parties are
requested to contact NAi Publishers, Mauritsweg 23,
3012 JR Rotterdam, The Netherlands.

Available in North, South and Central America through
D.A.P./Distributed Art Publishers Inc, 155 Sixth
Avenue 2nd Floor, New York, NY 10013-1507, Tel 212
6271999, Fax 212 6279484.

Available in the United Kingdom and Ireland through
Art Data, 12 Bell Industrial Estate, 50 Cunnington
Street, London W4 5HB, Tel 208 7471061, Fax 208
7422319.

Printed and bound in Belgium

ISSN 1570-4181
ISBN 978-90-5662-736-2